collectible glass
ROSE BOWLS

a history and identification guide
by Johanna S. Billings
with Sean Billings

collectible glass
ROSE BOWLS

a history and identification guide
by Johanna S. Billings
with Sean Billings

ANTIQUE TRADER BOOKS
A DIVISION OF LANDMARK SPECIALTY PUBLICATIONS
NORFOLK, VIRGINIA

White French piqué
Suit 1446

1446, of golden-brown shantung (without the coat)
Guimpe 1410, of China silk

Navy-blue chiffon panama
Suit 1421

Note the rose bowl on the table in this vintage clothing ad from
The Delineator *magazine. It is c. 1910.*

ISBN: 1-58221-009-08
Library of Congress Catalog Card Number: 1-99-61635

Editor: Sandra Holcombe
Art Director: Chris Decker
Assistant Editor: Wendy Chia-Klesch

Printed in the United States of America

To order additional copies of this book, or to obtain a catalog, please contact:

Antique Trader Books
P.O. Box 1050
Dubuque, Iowa 52004
1-800-334-7165
www.collect.com

CONTENTS

DEDICATION

For Kayleigh, who will one day inherit her parents' collection of heavenly orbs, and to the members of the Rose Bowl Collectors club— many of whom supported and had faith in us long before this book was even proposed.

Georgie Anderson
Marie Anderson
Bambi J. Babbitt
Rose E. Beach
Jim and Marilyn Binter
Shirley S. Braibish
Dr. Carol Breslin
Barbara A. Chasse
Harriet Y. Clough
Carolyn Cosgrove
Roy Dawson
Lynn Diffenderfer
Helen Dudzic
Ruth J. Farrar
Frank M. Fenton
Tom and Luann Freeman
Charles Garman
Cheryl Gibson-Doyne
Eileen and Graham Greeley
Julie and Joseph Harris
Lee and Nancy Henninger
Steve Hetherington, Glasstiques
Michael Hill
Stu and Sally Horn
Barbara Jeffries
Irene L. Jones
Bev and Randy Jones
Anne K. Kaler
Amy Stirling Kendrick
Dorothy Ladd
Lorraine Lawlor
Barbara W. LeDuc
LaVonne Luethke
Marilyn Martin
Bob and Marjorie McCleskey
Emily W. Minton

April C. "Carolyn" Moser
Terri Mowrer
Kathy B. Murdie
Judy L. Paris
Heidi Parlato
Joanne M. Pellow
Barbara Perkins
Tom Price
Louis Racine, Riverview Antiques
Dayla M. Rainwater
Barbara M. Rasmussen, Turn of the
  Century Antiques
Beatrice Ray
Ralph, Rusty and Scott Roland,
  GlimmerGlass Antiques
Martha Ross
Alfred Russell
Gloria S. St. Germain
James L. Sapp
Barbara Scates
John and Katherine Schaefgen
Irmgard Schmidt
Ellen Schroy
Darlene Severn
Karen Shaker
Ruth Sparks
Louis O. St. Aubin, Jr., Brookside Antiques
Caroleen Standish
Frank B. Strovel, Jr.
Irene Marie Billow Troelstra
Darla K. Waegele
Ellen Waldroop
Miriam A. Walter
Fred Wishnie, Wishful Things
Cheryl Wyatt

ACKNOWLEDGMENTS

A book is never a solitary endeavor. Many people contribute, often without realizing it. My heartfelt thanks go to my glass mentors, Louis O. St. Aubin, Jr., of Brookside Antiques, and Ralph, Rusty, and Scott Roland, of GlimmerGlass Antiques, for patiently answering many, many questions—some of which must have seemed very basic to them. I look forward to more "information sponging" in the future. And, thanks to several Rose Bowl Collectors members, including Martha Ross, Carolyn Cosgrove, and Marilyn Martin for freely sharing their knowledge.

Thanks also to Gary Baldwin, author of *Moser Artistic Glass*, for giving me his opinion on a number of Moser and Bohemian rose bowls. It's helpful to confer with other glass researchers, and he made it especially easy.

I must thank the members of the online art glass discussion group (www.tias.com/RHA), who made much of my detective work easier, whether I was looking for an address for a glass company or the identification of a signature. I appreciate not only the answers, but the questions, which helped me to get a handle on what readers will want to know. Thanks, gang!

Once I found the answers I was looking for—or some of them anyway—writing articles for various trade and consumer publications helped me to process my discoveries and remember details. I owe special thanks to my writing mentors, Dr. Anne K. Kaler and Dr. Carol Breslin, both of Gwynedd-Mercy College, who helped me make the jump from newspaper reporting to freelance writing. They did so, I might add, by critiquing as many manuscripts outside of class as inside. Hopefully, along the way they didn't mind learning many obscure but no doubt fascinating details about glass, cats, and Star Trek.

Thanks goes to Rose Bowl Collectors member Stu Horn, who was always willing to help in any way he could, not only with the book, but also with the club newsletter. His energy, enthusiasm, and good humor many times made my life much easier. Because of Stu, I will never look at Chef Boy R Dee in quite the same way!

Thanks to Stu, and RBC members Martha Ross and Ruth Sparks for allowing me to photograph their extensive collections which, along with mine, make up the bulk of the illustrations in this book. Not only did Stu let me photograph his rose bowls and then go for a swim in his hot tub to relax, but he shot several rolls of new bowls he acquired before the manuscript was completed.

Thanks, also, to the many people and companies listed below who provided one or two photos, or who permitted me to photograph their rose bowls at shows. Not all of the bowls made it into the book, but I still appreciate the cooperation of Ar-Jo Antiques/ Horatio Antiques; Doug Babcock; Robert Bartholomew; Rose Beach; David Billings; Theresa Brantley; Brookside Antiques; Karen Comer; John Corl of the Elegant Glass Collectors Club; Howard and Leslie Diehl; Bruce Dooley and Evan Walker; Robert E. Eaton, Jr.; Elvid Antiques; Odie and Joan Fincham, Jr.; Dottie Freeman and Allan Teal; GlimmerGlass Antiques; Grandma Patty's Antiques; Bob Kretchko; Bob and Marjorie McCleskey; Larry and Kathy Murdie; Precious and Few; Arlene Rabin; Candace Reed; Riverview Antiques; Rose Colored Glass; Andy Schilero; Search Ends Here; Brian Severn; Shand Gallery; Irmgard Schmidt; Frank B. Strovel, Jr.; Ron Teal, Jr.; and others who asked to remain anonymous.

Last, but certainly not least, I would like to thank my husband, Sean, for all his hard work with the photographs, compiling pricing and pattern data, proofreading, and humoring me—especially when I decided I had to have an Egg McMuffin at 6 a.m. after staying up all night working! Although I did the writing, he did a lot of the work that made the writing possible.

AUTHOR'S NOTE

Picture book or scholarly work? They say those are the two kinds of books. Among the masters in this business, only the second kind counts. So, in a very real sense, there is pressure on me to make this a scholarly work. Because I have pride in my work, I want it to count, too.

I haven't been at this as long as many in the field. I remember a time not too long ago when I read the scholarly works of my peers and words like "Pomona" and "Vasa Murrhina" meant nothing to me. I went to other sources to find definitions and descriptions of these terms, but often after consulting several works, these terms still meant nothing to me. The only things which brought such terms into focus were pictures.

For the novice or new collector, there must be pictures. Lots of pictures. And for the glass collecting field to survive, there must be new collectors. So I will make no apologies for including lots of pictures in this book. Writers are always told by their teachers and mentors, "Don't tell me. Show me." When writing a book about a shape which has so many variations in form, color, size, and decoration, pictures save me from writing thousands of words which can be taken a thousand different ways by a thousand different readers. And, thus, a picture book has its place.

However, my hope is that this book will serve not only novices but intermediate and advanced collectors and dealers. My favorite references are those with many layers of meaning which can be read over and over as the reader gains knowledge and experience, offering many new insights at each reading. I hope this is a book like that. I think it definitely has that potential, since much of the information included in these pages applies to other shapes as well as to rose bowls. Even if you don't collect rose bowls, I hope this will be a valuable reference for you.

Hopes aside, this book will differ from other references in important ways. Although I hope to be scholarly, I am not including lists of names of factory workers, detailed histories of companies, or glass formula ingredients. There are a number of reasons. First of all, it would take volumes to provide that kind of information on all the different companies that made rose bowls. Second, much of that information is available elsewhere. Third, as a collector, my primary interest is the age and identity of the piece before me. I will concentrate my efforts in this book to answer those kinds of questions.

I am including practical information on my observations and experience with this shape to show you not only what is known about a piece, but what also could be eventually proven true. In some cases, I'll be proven wrong. That's OK, as long as what I've written causes you, the reader, to think.

I'm not here to give you all the answers. I have relatively few. Instead, I hope to cause you to consider many details about this shape which you may have overlooked before, so that you may form your own conclusions, or at least gain an idea of how and where to find the answers to your questions.

—Johanna S. Billings

INTRODUCTION

What is a rose bowl? Ah! The regal beauty of rose bowls! Who can resist? Certainly not the author! Nor can many other collectors. Unfortunately, finding information on these simple but elegant pieces has not been nearly as easy as falling in love with them. That's what led me to write *Collectible Glass Rose Bowls*—so I could give collectors and dealers a practical, easy-to-use reference book.

Before going any further, I think it is important to clear up some of the confusion over what is, and is not, a rose bowl. As this shape has gained more and more notice in recent years, dealers have begun calling anything and everything a "rose bowl." This is no more correct than referring to a cruet as a "whiskey decanter" or a "pitcher"—worse, in fact, since some of these things people are calling rose bowls aren't even close.

A rose bowl generally is a round piece which turns in at the top, but does not turn up or back out again. Most have crimps, but pieces which have smooth or scalloped rims can also be considered rose bowls as long as they turn inward, but do not turn up or back out.

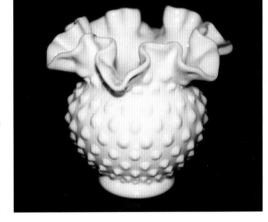

The problem arises from the fact that manufacturers sometimes used the term "rose bowl" to describe pieces which do not fit this definition. It would be wrong to go so far as to say these are not rose bowls. If that's what the manufacturer called them, that's what they are.

However, that doesn't mean that just because one manufacturer called, say, a double crimp vase a "rose bowl," that all double crimp vases are actually rose bowls. I want to be true to manufacturer labels, but I want to be true to the shape, also. Therefore, I suggest that when a piece does not meet the above definition, but is nevertheless called a "rose bowl"—by the manufacturer—we should note it as: "Rose bowl only according to the manufacturer's catalog."

Fenton, for example, in a 1939 catalog uses the term "rose bowl" for a wide range of crystal shapes in its 201 line. Only one or two examples in this line-up would meet the accepted definition. So, to avoid confusing everyone, I believe that it would be safer and more accurate to describe the shapes as they are, making note of Fenton's

Fig. 1. This Fenton milk glass hobnail piece is not a rose bowl. It is referred to in old catalogs as a "double crimp vase."

descriptions. This is especially important in this case because Fenton did not stop with the term "rose bowl" when naming these other shapes. The complete names of the "cup flared rose bowl," "cup triangle rose bowl" and "pinched rose bowl" give at least some indication that these are not what one would typically refer to as a rose bowl.

Heisey also uses the term "rose bowl" to describe what I would call a compote in its Sahara line. This item stands on a pedestal base and turns outward, with a folded-down edge at the top. It should be noted that this is a rose bowl only according to Heisey catalogs. Referring to this piece as a rose bowl, without making note of the fact that, in this case, the term "rose bowl" is simply the manufacturer's own term for the piece, only causes confusion.

It's also important to note that Europe has a completely different definition of a "rose bowl." In Germany and Holland, for example, the term "rose bowl" refers to a low bulbous shape with a small neck for accommodating a metal grid for flower arrangements. The crimped shape we Americans know as a rose bowl has no real equivalent in Europe, says Dutch glass collector Ivo Haanstra, and Europeans would likely designate our rose bowls as "potpourri vases."

"Flower vases for hyacinths, carnations, tulips, freesias, and roses are found in nearly every household, and most antique dealers will name them correctly. Most rose vases with a little grid were made in Bohemia and in England; the cut crystal variety was made in Holland, Belgium, and Germany. The grid is very often missing; it tends to get thrown out with the flowers," writes Ivo.

"The bowl of potpourri on the mantel piece was kept in a potpourri jar, sometimes called a pomander vase. Potpourri jars are found in porcelain, but hardly ever in glass. No wonder you didn't see rose bowls in Holland—they're practically absent. You will find them in England, though, and in France, both full size and miniature. French antique dealers will refer to these as vases; only very rarely will anyone recognize them for what they are, namely a 'parfumer' or 'bol parfumeur'."

Although there is a wide variety of shapes outside the definition given at the beginning of this section that are called "rose bowls" by the manufacturers, they are beyond the scope of this book. There is no way to do justice to them all, so the book will cover only those which meet the above definition.

You will, no doubt, also notice that the emphasis of this book is on crimped rose bowls. This is not done in an effort to slight those rose bowls that are not crimped. But virtually all rose bowl collectors agree that a spherical piece that turns in at the top, and is crimped, is indeed a rose bowl. In fact, this is often called the "classic style." Once you start discussing pieces that are not crimped, or which are taller than they are wide, or wider than they are tall, or vary in some other way from that classic style, collectors begin to disagree over whether the piece is really a rose bowl. These variations will be covered somewhat throughout this book, but the core focus will be on those examples that are shaped in the classic style. The closer to the classic style they are, the more coverage they will receive in these pages. The more they deviate from that classic style, the less emphasis they will receive. Let's face it: The research for any book has to end somewhere. This seemed as fair a place as any to draw the line.

Origin and History of the Rose Bowl

This shape first appeared in cut and pressed glass in the late nineteenth century. The earliest I have been able to document is 1880, though Charles R. Hajdamach, in his book *British Glass: 1800-1914*, notes that crimping began to be popular in Britain in 1874; so it's possible that spherical vessels were crimped in the 1870s, creating the shape we now know as the rose bowl.

Rose bowls were made in both Europe and the United States by virtually every glass manufacturer, and in practically every type of glass. Rose bowls peaked in popularity in the late Victorian era, but they are still being made today by a handful of companies.

The rose bowl was purported to serve as a vase or a container for homemade potpourri. Some speculate that crimped tops were intended to support the heavy blooms of what we would, today, call antique roses. This might very well be true since long-stemmed roses are a modern invention. The roses of the nineteenth century were hardier and short-stemmed, with heavy, dense blooms. Regardless, rose bowls provided a splash of bright color in contrast with often dark Victorian decor.

No one is really sure where the name "rose bowl" came from. One advanced collector says they were originally called "flower bowls" and gradually became known as "rose bowls" because they were used to hold roses. This might also be true since, as discussed earlier, manufacturer names for this shape vary widely, and names, styles, and colors were invented according to what would sell.

We do know that the term "rose bowl" was in use by 1894, when Consolidated Lamp and Glass Company, operating in Fostoria, Ohio, apparently found this shape to be a commercial success. "There are quite a number of new things in rose bowls that will catch the eyes of the ladies," notes the December 12, 1894, issue of *China Glass & Lamps*. "It is worth mentioning that when the Consolidated people made their first rose bowls, it was without any intention of adding them to their lines of goods regularly made; but they sold so well that they are now considered staples, and they make lots of them."

Fig. 2. This Crown Milano piece also is not a rose bowl, since it turns in but then up at the top.

Fig. 3. This piece with its wire mesh top, is what people in Europe call a "rose bowl."

The May 8, 1895, issue of that same publication also makes note of Consolidated's rose bowls, writing: "The showing of knick knacks in the way of jardiniers, rose bowls, vases, flower tubes and the like is increasingly attractive."

Rose bowls remained quite popular through about 1920, when their popularity waned. Still, a few were made in America, and quite a few were made in other parts of the world during the Great Depression and beyond. Although the rose bowl has never made a full comeback, its popularity does seem to be increasing, judging by the number of rose bowls showing up in retail stores.

Rose Bowl Forms and Features

It's a lot easier to follow a discussion of what makes one rose bowl different from another if you know the terminology used to describe them.

Crimps: This term is used to describe the wavy top of most rose bowls. It somewhat resembles the edge of a fluted pie crust.

Box pleat: A rather square crimp style in which the crimps are wider than tall, and squared at each end. Stevens & Williams of England is the only known maker of box pleated glass (see figs. 100 and 101).

Scalloped: The wavy or notched pattern around the opening of a rose bowl that is not crimped. This style opening is often found in pattern and Depression glass (see figs. 294 and 416 for two different examples).

Collar foot: Also called a "wafer foot," this is a short round base on which the bulbous bottom of a rose bowl sits. It looks kind of like a cookie underneath the bowl. This type of foot is common on Fenton and Wright rose bowls (see fig. 420).

Pedestal base: A taller foot, which makes the rose bowl stand up, as if it were the top of a goblet (see fig. 259).

Egg shaped: Used to describe a rose bowl that is taller than it is wide (see fig. 68).

Squat: A term used to describe a rose bowl that is wider than it is tall. It is also used to describe rose bowls that have flattened, in-turned crimps (see fig. 81).

Rose bowl basket: A handled rose bowl, generally with a crimped top (see fig. 182).

Rough pontil: One that is left unfinished, and not ground or polished. Sometimes also referred to as an "open pontil." For those not familiar with pontil marks, these are the scars left on the bottom of the piece by the pontil rod—not by the blowpipe, as some mistakenly believe—a tool used in finishing (see fig. 571). Pressed pieces do not have any pontil marks.

Ground pontil: One that has been ground smooth (see fig. 137).

Polished pontil: One that has been ground smooth and then polished so that it is as clear and smooth as the rest of the piece (see fig. 194). It is important to note that the pontil mark has nothing to do with age. The mark appears on brand new items as well as on much older pieces.

Prunt: A decorative glob of applied glass, sometimes applied over a pontil (see figs. 327 and 339).

chapter one

VICTORIAN GLASS ROSE BOWLS
1880-1910

Since rose bowls experienced their heyday in the late Victorian era, this is the most colorful period—literally—in their history. The Victorians were well known for their lavishness. One of anything was never enough, and glassmakers were only too happy to produce things like rose bowls to fill endless nooks, crannies, and knickknack shelves which simply could not be left empty.

The endless variety of rose bowls produced meant that there was a rose bowl, or several, to fit every budget. In fact, a woman was not considered to be properly set up for housekeeping without one.

Rose bowls can be found in satin, mother-of-pearl satin, Burmese, peachblow, opalescent, spatter and spangled glass, among others. Brightly colored art glass rose bowls provided a refreshing splash of color, contrasting well with the often dark colors used in home furnishings during this period.

The scope of this book is not broad enough to discuss each type of Victorian glass in detail. The book will provide an overview of glass made during the period with emphasis on the types in which the collector is most likely to find rose bowls. Some Victorian glass types of lesser importance to rose bowl collectors will be covered in photo captions.

Many good books exist on Victorian art glass in general, specific types of Victorian glass such as opalescent, and the products of particular companies. The books listed in the bibliography are recommended for those who wish to acquire more in-depth knowledge.

Before getting into specific types of glass, it is important to note that not all rose bowls are created equal. Although they share the same general shape, minute but important variations in shape do exist and these provide clues to a rose bowl's origin. Some have taller crimps than others. Some are narrower at the bottom than at the top or vice versa. Some have bases and others do not. Sometimes you must look very closely to even see these differences, but once you do, you will begin to learn to recognize these characteristics and how they can be helpful in attribution. Each subsection of this book will discuss the subtle characteristics present in each type of glass along with what these characteristics say about their origins of the pieces in question.

1.1. Satin and Mother-of-Pearl Satin

Rose bowls were made extensively in satin glass, which is an opaque or semi-opaque colored ware, usually lined in white, which has a soft and silky matte finish, thanks to a bath in hydrofluoric acid. Rose bowls in pink, powder blue, and yellow satin glass are the most common, followed by other colors such as green, purple, apricot, brown, and rainbow.

Some are even found with glossy finishes. I don't know if there was a specific name for this kind of glass. I usually refer to it as "glossy satin," since the rose bowls found with glossy finishes are otherwise identical to their matte-finished counterparts. So far, I have seen them only in pink, blue, and yellow. Glossy satin rose bowls are much less common than matte ones, although there is really no corresponding difference in value.

Having peaked in popularity from the 1880s through the turn of the century, satin glass rose bowls were made by such companies as Thomas Webb & Sons, and Stevens & Williams, in England, and by Mt. Washington, and Consolidated, in the United States. Some rose bowls were also made in other parts of Europe, most notably Bohemia, in what is now the Czech Republic.

Incidentally, you will notice that I usually refer to Thomas Webb & Sons as "Thomas Webb," rather than just "Webb." That's because three different British glass companies include "Webb" as a part of their name. It is more correct to refer to the glass as made by "Thomas Webb" rather than just "Webb."

Although satin glass was generally left unmarked, that doesn't mean it is never marked. The acid stamp "MADE IN BOHEMIA" can sometimes be found on the bottom of Bohemian satin rose bowls. It's faint, so look closely at the pontil area. This mark looks like a stamp surrounding the actual pontil scar. A close study of the shape of these signed rose bowls has allowed me to take a leap of faith and say that other rose bowls sharing this size and shape are Bohemian. Thomas Webb rose bowls are also sometimes marked.

Though many are undecorated, satin rose bowls are often found with enameled, gilded, or painted decorations. Most companies used more than one decorative design on a given rose bowl shape. Some even have designs blown out or "embossed" into the glass, provid-

Fig. 4. Common pink, blue, and yellow rose bowls. Note the minor shape variations. The blue one, and possibly the yellow one, could be Mt. Washington. Author's collection.

Fig. 5. Glossy "satin" rose bowls that never got their acid bath. Possibly Mt. Washington. Author's collection.

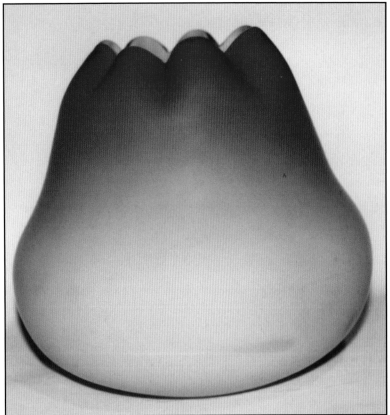

Fig. 6. A pink satin rose bowl in an unusual shape. Courtesy of GlimmerGlass Antiques.

ing an effect much like that of a notary seal. These designs include shells and florals primarily, although ribbing, berries, and foliage are also found.

Mother-of-pearl satin, also called Pearl Satin, Pearlware, or MOP satin, is a beautiful variation of satin glass, which uses air trapped between layers of glass to form the pattern. Generally, the inside layer was blown into a mold to create the pattern. When an outer layer of glass was added, air trapped between the layers of glass created the pattern.

Like regular satin glass, the colors most commonly found in mother-of-pearl satin are pink, powder blue, and yellow—with yellow being the most common of the three. But mother-of-pearl satin glass rose bowls were also made in many of the same colors in which plain satin rose bowls are found, including purple, rainbow, and even white.

The most common pattern in mother-of-pearl satin is diamond quilted, followed by herringbone. This ware was also made in a multitude of other patterns such as raindrop, swirl, moiré, and peacock eye. Although those patterns are much more scarce, rose bowls were made in these patterns, so look carefully!

Mother-of-pearl satin was made by many of the same companies that made regular satin glass. In England, it is not called mother-of-pearl, but "airtrap" glass.

It is difficult, but not impossible, to attribute the origins of satin and mother-of-pearl satin glass rose bowls. Those made by Thomas Webb, for example, have several distinctive shapes, which can be attributed through decoration, glass types in which they are found, and documentation in other published sources. The Webb rose bowl shape seen most often is perfectly spherical, with eight softly rounded crimps. The pontils on these usually show a cross section of the different layers of glass. These characteristics are true whether the rose bowl is satin, mother-of-pearl satin, crimped mother-of-pearl satin cameo, peachblow, or even Burmese (although Burmese glass is single layered, so obviously only one type of glass is visible in the pontil).

Other rose bowl shapes known to be Thomas Webb include a small tri-crimped style on a short wafer foot, and a squat shape with nine pointed crimps which turn in only slightly. Most of the time, these are seen in mother-of-pearl satin, but on occasion, you can find them in regular satin glass. The pontils on these are different than on their spherical counterparts. The layers of glass don't show through as a set of concentric circles on the pontils of these bowls as they do on the spherical ones.

Stevens & Williams satin and mother-of-pearl satin rose bowls can be identified through the box pleat, which is the company's squared form of crimping. Not all Stevens &

Fig 7. Purple is one of the most desirable colors in satin glass. Attributed to Mt. Washington. Author's collection.

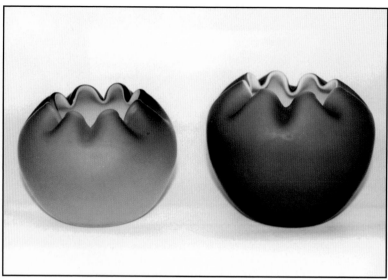

Fig. 8. More purple satin rose bowls. Author's collection.

Fig. 9. Turquoise satin doesn't have the shading usually seen on satin rose bowls. Author's collection.

Fig. 10. Note the translucence on these two, believed to be Bohemian because the glass is the same as found on known Bohemian rose bowls. Author's collection.

Williams rose bowls have box pleats, but those that do can be attributed, as can those without a box pleat found in the same shapes or glass treatments as those with the box pleat. Stevens & Williams had a patent for box pleats, and no other company is known to have made them. Likewise, we can attribute Stevens & Williams rose bowl shapes that don't have box pleats when the shape or style of glass is also found with the box pleats. This company did perfectly spherical rose bowls, as well as some rose bowls which are squat or egg-shaped.

One more clue to identification is the word "PATENT" found on the bottom of some satin and mother-of-pearl satin rose bowls. Rose bowls that are found with this mark are generally English.

Like those made by Thomas Webb, Mt. Washington rose bowls also have a distinctive shape, which is discussed in the next section because this shape occurs most often in the company's Lusterless, Albertine, and Crown Milano lines. A few rose bowls in shapes other than those found in the lines named above have been attributed to Mt. Washington based on shape, colors, and glass shards found at the former factory site. In satin glass, the rose bowls attributed to Mt. Washington have ground pontils and eight indented lines in the glass which swirl counterclockwise from top to bottom. The enameling on these is usually lovely and well-done.

I also believe a number of egg-style satin rose bowls can be attributed to Mt. Washington. We know that Mt. Washington made egg-style rose bowls in its Lusterless glass (see figs. 124 and 125). If you compare the design on this known Mt. Washington rose bowl to designs found on egg-shaped rose bowls in other colors, you'll see a striking similarity. The decoration on fig. 65 is nearly identical to that on fig. 124.

We can take it a step farther by comparing the decorative styles to the style on fig. 66, which also is likely to be Mt. Washington. Likewise, compare the decorative style on fig. 68 to the styles of known Mt. Washington rose bowls, such as fig. 148.

It gets more interesting yet. If the decorated egg-style rose bowl is Mt. Washington, then surely the undecorated one next to it is Mt. Washington. The shape is identical, as is the

Fig. 11. Trio of olive satin miniatures, 2" to 2-1/2" high. Probably English. Collection of Martha Ross.

Fig. 12. Raspberry satin enameled. This shape is also seen in periwinkle blue and custard. Author's collection (see fig. 17).

Fig. 13. Blue satin enameled also found in pink and yellow, attributed to Mt. Washington. Author's collection.

Fig. 14. Unusual unshaded yellow enameled rose bowl. Author's collection.

Fig. 15. Pink enameled rose bowl. Author's collection.

Fig. 16. Apricot satin rose bowl, probably Bohemian. Author's collection.

Fig. 17. Unshaded periwinkle blue enameled rose bowl, obviously made by the same company that made the one shown in fig. 12. Periwinkle blue is much less common than raspberry satin. Author's collection.

Fig. 18. Mint green uncased enameled satin rose bowl, also seen in a mint blue and raspberry. It was probably made by the same company that made the ones in figs. 12 and 17. Author's collection.

shape in the glossy one in fig. 67. Now compare the color of fig. 67 with the blue one shown in fig. 5. I've also seen yellow and pink glossy egg-shaped rose bowls whose colors exactly match the pink and yellow rose bowls in fig. 5.

Let's go back to shape for a minute. If the rose bowls in fig. 5 are Mt. Washington, then the large blue bowl and possibly the yellow one in fig. 4 are also Mt. Washington. Likewise, figures 7, 13, 21, 22, and 48 would then be Mt. Washington. What's interesting about this is that I have had experts suggest to me that figures 21 and 22 were Mt. Washington before I even began this line of thinking—thereby connecting all these rose bowls together. So, there's a good chance I'm right!

Mt. Washington did do cherub designs on their glass, though I don't have proof that they used this design on rose bowls. If they did, then certainly even more rose bowls could be attributed to Mt. Washington. This would stand to reason since a lot of egg-style rose bowls have the cherub design. The cherub-decorated bowl, fig. 373, also certainly exhibits the Mt. Washington shape. It's also possible that Mt. Washington made the blanks, and that they were subsequently decorated elsewhere.

No matter how you slice it, I'm going out on a limb, here. You must realize that this is strictly my opinion, and not proven fact, although the argument certainly has merit. That's why I have identified these bowls as "attributed to Mt. Washington," rather than simply stating "Mt. Washington." It's quite possible I'll eventually be proven wrong. Which leads me to a quote by one of my mentors, Louis O. St. Aubin, Jr.—a quote I believe everyone should remember when analyzing and attributing glass: **"The longer I'm in this business, the more I realize that these things (attributions) are subject to interpretation."**

Interestingly, mother-of-pearl satin rose bowls attributed to Mt. Washington don't meet the same standards of quality found in the company's other lines. Of the two American companies to make this type of glass, Phoenix did a better job than Mt. Washington. Crimps and pontils on Mt. Washington rose bowls tend to be less uniform than those found on other mother-of-pearl satin rose bowls. If you take the shape analysis from this point, you could make even more Mt. Washington attributions!

I am much more certain about the attribution of Shell & Seaweed rose bowls, made by Consolidated Lamp & Glass Company. Both William Heacock and Mel Murray made this attribution before me. We also know from the Victorian-era trade publication, *China Glass & Lamps*, that Consolidated made a lot of rose bowls. And, if you pay attention to Consolidated's line, you'll see that the company made a lot of blown-out or embossed patterns.

Fig. 19. Small blue satin, simply enameled.

Fig. 20. Factory painted green satin with swirls in the glass. Author's collection.

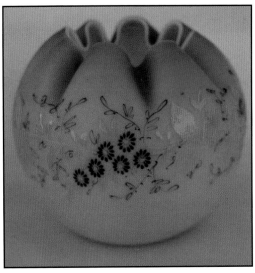

Fig. 21. This enameled rose bowl, with indented swirls in the glass, is marked "Xmas 1894" on the bottom. I have seen it in yellow, and assume it is also found in blue, and possibly green and purple. Attributed to Mt. Washington. 5" tall. Author's collection.

Fig. 22. This one is attributed to Mt. Washington since it is identical in shape and size to fig. 21. Mt. Washington often did little enameled daisies like those on this one. Note the difference in color on this one and fig. 20. Author's collection.

I believe it's possible that Consolidated can be credited with the creation of other embossed designs like the "Cabbage Rose." The general shape and crimp style of these three patterns are strikingly similar.

Of course, the pitfall to this line of thinking is that Consolidated's crimps look very much like those on some Bohemian rose bowls. Still, it's the closest anyone has come to attributing the Cabbage Rose or any embossed satin rose bowls.

If Consolidated made the Shell & Seaweed pattern, and only Mt. Washington and Phoenix made mother-of-pearl satin glass in America, then how is it that Shell & Seaweed rose bowls are found in mother-of-pearl satin? The exact details are cloudy, but apparently Phoenix and Consolidated were connected through common investors and the exchange of molds. It makes sense then that a Consolidated pattern would show up in Phoenix mother-of-pearl satin.

I have also seen some diamond quilted mother-of-pearl satin rose bowls attributed to Stevens & Williams by top dealers in the business. Certainly their opinions have merit. These rose bowls are thicker than mother-of-pearl satin by other companies (see figs. 69 and 72). Stevens & Williams Pompeiian Swirl pattern, on the other hand, is not thick at all. Another pitfall to this line of thinking is that Americans tend to attribute everything English to Thomas Webb or Stevens & Williams. I am stopping short of making the same attribution because it would be based on hearsay, even though those who've made the attribution are highly respected.

In addition to mother-of-pearl satin, there is a form called cut velvet, which is characterized by a raised pattern instead of an airtrap pattern. Mt. Washington had a patent on this treatment, though other companies certainly could have copied it.

Satin and mother-of-pearl satin rose bowls have been reproduced. For in-depth information on reproductions and how to tell the difference, see sections 3.2 and 3.4.

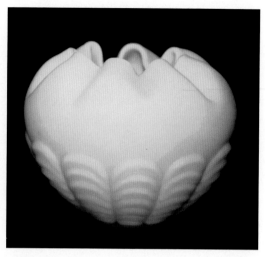

Fig. 24. Custard Fan Embossed. Collection of Stu Horn.

Fig. 23. The manufacturer and pattern name is unknown, but Rose Bowl Collectors have nicknamed it "Fan Embossed." Found only in undecorated turquoise, raspberry and custard. 3-1/2" high. Author's collection.

Fig. 25. This is one of the few glossy "satin" rose bowls to be found decorated. Standing 2-1/2" high, it comes in pink, blue, and yellow. Other colors possible. Author's collection.

Fig. 26. Turquoise Fan Embossed. Collection of David Billings.

Fig. 27. Purple Cabbage Rose. Author's collection.

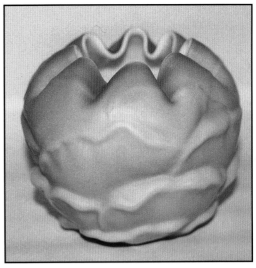

Fig. 28. Pink Cabbage Rose. Author's collection.

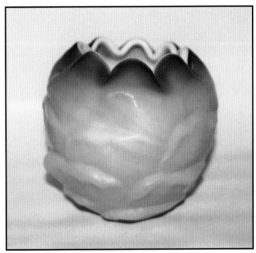

Fig. 30. Green Cabbage Rose. Author's collection.

Fig. 29. This style, nicknamed "Cabbage Rose" by collectors, is one of the most popular. It comes in pink, blue, yellow, green, and purple. 4" high. Author's and Stu Horn's collections.

Fig. 31. Often attributed to Mt. Washington, the Shell Embossed pattern comes in pink, blue, yellow, and white. The actual manufacturer is unknown. Collection of Stu Horn.

Fig. 32. Not only is this pattern rare in white, and rare decorated, but it stands about a half-inch shorter than the blue, pink, and yellow examples. Collection of Stu Horn.

Fig. 33. Close-up of pink Shell Embossed rose bowl. 4" high. Author's collection.

Fig. 34. Shell & Seaweed, made by the Consolidated Lamp & Glass Co., c. 1894, comes in 3-1/2" and 5" sizes in pink, blue, yellow, green, and purple. This one is the larger size, in green. Author's collection.

Fig. 35. Small enameled blue Shell & Seaweed. Author's collection.

Fig. 37. Large pink enameled Shell & Seaweed. Author's collection.

Fig. 36. Large purple Shell & Seaweed. Author's collection.

Fig. 38. Small undecorated yellow satin Shell & Seaweed. Author's collection.

Fig. 39. Note the differences in crimp style and shape between the Shell Embossed (left) and Shell & Seaweed. Note also the absence of ribbing on the Shell & Seaweed pattern, and the absence of the seaweed in the Shell Embossed. Author's collection.

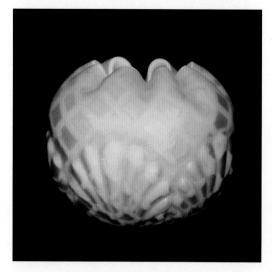

Fig. 40. The mother-of-pearl satin Shell & Seaweed rose bowls must have been made by Phoenix. Consolidated is not known to have made mother-of-pearl satin. Collection of Stu Horn.

Fig. 41. Although not made of satin glass, this rare rubena verde Shell & Seaweed rose bowl is shown here, with others in the same pattern. Collection of Stu Horn.

Fig. 42. The maker and original manufacturer name of the blown out Floral Embossed rose bowls are uncertain. However, they are the same size and basic shape as the Shell & Seaweed, and have a similar crimp style. They're found in pink, blue, yellow, green, and purple. Author's collection.

Fig. 43. Blue Floral Embossed. Photo courtesy of David and Irmgard Schmidt.

Fig. 44. Unlined ribbed satin rose bowls are found in pink, blue, and an off-white. Only the white ones are found decorated. 3" high. Collection of Stu Horn.

Fig. 45. Close-up of off-white enameled ribbed satin. Collection of Stu Horn.

Fig. 46. Note the finely enameled decoration, believed to be Bohemian. Applied glass toes aren't common on satin rose bowls, but they aren't unheard of either. Collection of Stu Horn.

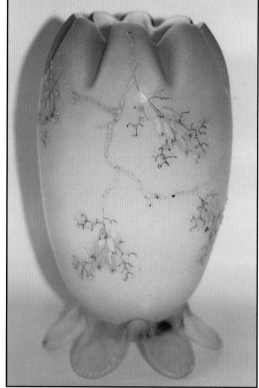

Fig. 47. Tall, toed, Bohemian satin rose bowl. Collection of Martha Ross.

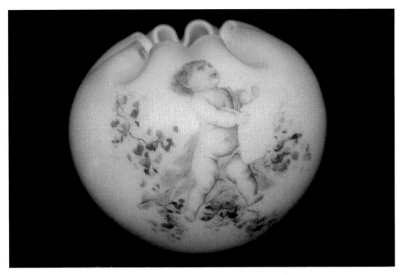

Fig. 48. *Cherub decals are found on pink, blue, and yellow rose bowls, in both spherical and egg shapes. The cherub designs vary, with some showing more than one cherub. This one attributed to Mt. Washington. Author's collection.*

Fig. 49. *Most souvenir rose bowls seem to be from either Bohemia or Austria. So, these Niagara Falls souvenir rose bowls were also probably made there. Collection of Frank B. Strovel, Jr.*

Fig. 51. *Another Niagara Falls souvenir rose bowl. Photo courtesy of David and Irmgard Schmidt.*

Fig. 50. *Note the differences between this Niagara Falls souvenir and the others. Author's collection.*

Fig. 52. Imagine going to a gift shop and being able to buy a souvenir like this, instead of a cheap cedar box or plastic trinket. This rose bowl is stamped "MADE IN BOHEMIA" around the pontil. It is enameled "A Present from London." The Bohemians made these to be sold as souvenirs from a variety of locations in the British Isles. Author's collection.

Fig. 53. Another souvenir rose bowl, this one of St. Augustine's city gates. Collection of Ruth Sparks.

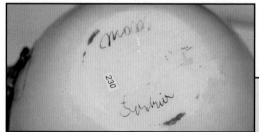

Fig. 54. The mark is difficult to read, but apparently it reads, "Austria."

Fig. 55. This souvenir bowl from a pier on the sea, has a nearly illegible signature on the bottom. Author's collection.

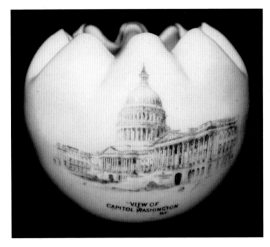

Fig. 56. Even souvenirs of U.S. locations were imported. This souvenir from the U.S. Capitol Building is marked "Austria." Author's collection.

Fig. 57. Mark on bottom of fig. 56.

Fig. 58. This unusual four-crimped shape comes in blue, yellow, pink, and apricot. It is not marked, but may very well be Bohemian since known Bohemian rose bowls in other types of glass are found in this shape. Author's collection.

Fig. 59. This souvenir is not Bohemian. It was made by Libbey at the 1893 World's Fair. Collection of Ruth Sparks.

Fig. 60. Brown satin is one of the most rare and desirable colors in rose bowls. This is an example of the work of Thomas Webb and Jules Barbe. Collection of Ruth Sparks.

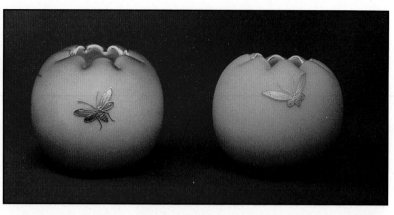

Fig. 61. Many debates have been held about the significance of butterflies on glass by Thomas Webb. The only significance thus far documented is their decorative value. These are often found on the back sides of those with gilded Jules Barbe decorations. Photo courtesy of Bob & Marjorie McCleskey.

Fig. 62. That perfectly spherical Thomas Webb shape shows in these blue satin, diamond-quilted, mother-of-pearl rose bowls with applied glass flowers, which unfortunately are seldom found intact. Collection of Stu Horn.

Fig. 63. This slightly egg-shaped, four-crimped, herringbone, mother-of-pearl is the work of Thomas Webb & Sons. Note the striking similarities of the flowers. This shape is also a Webb shape. Collection of Stu Horn.

Fig. 64. There's no mistaking the exceptional work of Thomas Webb & Sons of England. This blue satin example stands only 2" high and has Jules Barbe's gilded Prunus decoration. Author's collection.

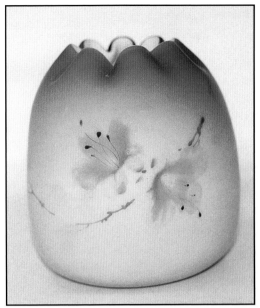

Fig. 66. Pink satin egg style, 4". Attributed to Mt. Washington. Collection of Martha Ross.

Fig. 65. This yellow example can be attributed to Mt. Washington because this design is also found on the company's Lusterless egg-shaped rose bowls (see fig. 124). Collection of David Billings.

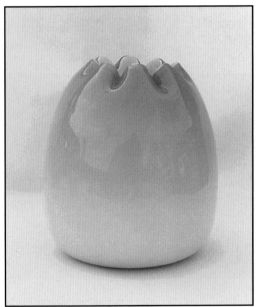

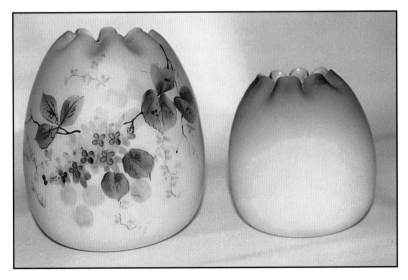

Fig. 67. Egg-style rose bowls were also made in glossy "satin." Possibly Mt. Washington. Author's collection.

Left: Fig. 68. Rose bowls in this classic egg shape are found in pink, blue, and yellow. They were made in two sizes and are found both with and without decorations. Attributed to Mt. Washington. Author's collection.

Fig. 69. *Shaded rose satin diamond quilted mother-of-pearl miniature, standing 2-1/2" tall. It has a concave ground pontil and is marked "PATENT," indicating it is English. I have seen rose bowls in this shape attributed to Stevens & Williams by top dealers in the business. Note that the glass is rather thick for Victorian mother-of-pearl. Author's collection.*

Fig. 70. *This blue satin diamond quilted mother-of-pearl example shows off the Thomas Webb shape. 3-3/4" high. Author's collection.*

Fig. 71. *White and off-white are rare colors in mother-of-pearl satin glass. This exquisite example is by Thomas Webb & Sons. 3" high. Author's collection.*

Fig. 72. *The ultimate in rose bowl collecting has to be a miniature rainbow satin mother-of-pearl example like this one, marked "PATENT." 2-1/2" high. Author's collection.*

Fig. 73. *Another rainbow mother-of-pearl example. Photo by Bill Pitt, courtesy of Brookside Antiques.*

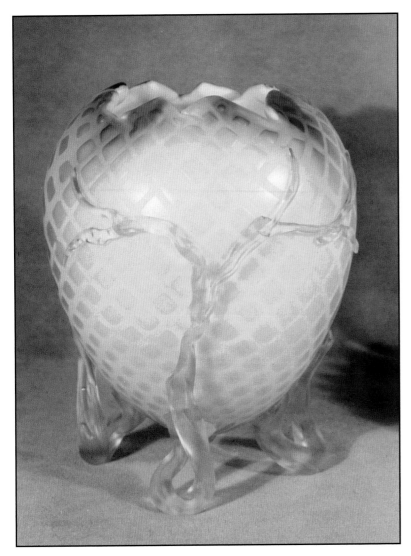

Fig. 74. This rainbow diamond quilted mother-of-pearl example shows an unusual "dinosaur egg" style opening, and an egg shape, along with applied glass feet. Photo by Bill Pitt, courtesy of Brookside Antiques.

Fig. 75. Blue herringbone mother-of-pearl rose bowl. Collection of Stu Horn.

Fig. 76. It looks all apricot at first glance, but there is actually a rainbow of colors towards the base. I have seen this shape attributed to Thomas Webb, though I am uncertain if that is the case. Collection of Stu Horn.

Fig. 77. Pink herringbone mother-of-pearl. 3-3/8" high. Author's collection.

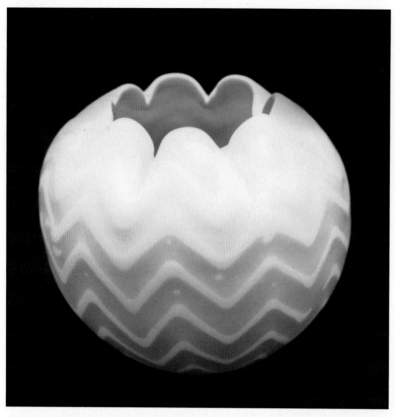

Fig. 78. *White herringbone mother-of-pearl satin with pink interior. 3-5/8" high, rough pontil. Attributed to Mt. Washington. Author's collection.*

Fig. 79. *Apricot herringbone mother-of-pearl satin. Photo courtesy of David and Irmgard Schmidt.*

Fig. 80. *Pontil on 81.*

Fig. 81. *Pink ribbon mother-of-pearl satin. This shape is typically thought to be Thomas Webb. Author's collection.*

Fig. 82. *White satin ribbon mother-of-pearl example by Thomas Webb. Collection of Martha Ross.*

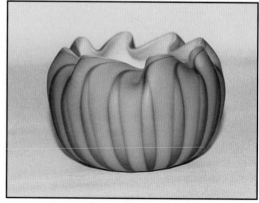

Fig. 83. *Gold Webb ribbon mother-of-pearl. Collection of Ruth Sparks.*

Fig. 84. Blue Webb ribbon mother-of-pearl with Coralene (not sure if it's authentic) decoration. Photo courtesy of Stu Horn.

Fig. 85. Here's another rose bowl shape found in ribbon mother-of-pearl. Collection of Ruth Sparks.

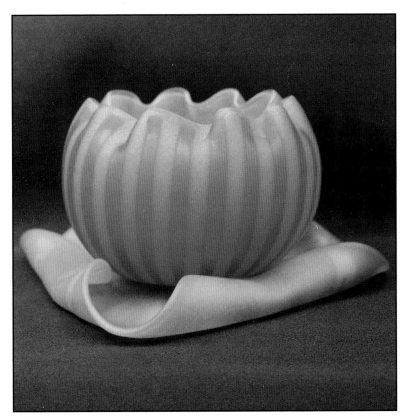

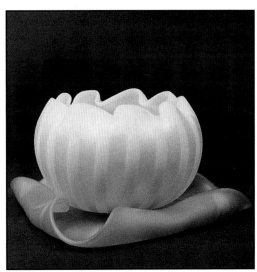

Fig. 87. An early reference book on art glass stated that white was the only known color in ribbon mother-of-pearl rose bowls. We know better now. Photo courtesy of Bob and Marjorie McCleskey.

Fig. 86. Sometimes squat ribbon mother-of-pearl rose bowls are found on bases that look something like lily pads. Some even have mirrors under their bases. Photo courtesy of Bob and Marjorie McCleskey.

Fig. 88. This Webb shape is found in both decorated and undecorated ribbon mother-of-pearl. This particular rose bowl has Jules Barbe's gilded decoration. Courtesy of Riverview Antiques.

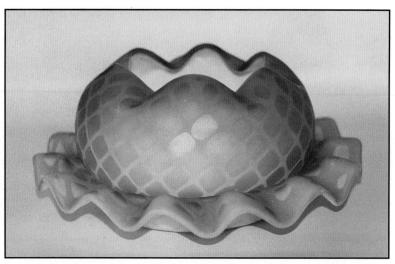

Fig. 89. Some people argue that this is a finger bowl, rather than a rose bowl. Most finger bowls, however, are part of a table set. Few, if any, table sets exist in mother-of-pearl satin. If it is a finger bowl, the crimps surely caused a few spills by catching the user's fingertips. Whatever you call this design, rose bowl collectors usually manage to get at least one in their collections. Collection of Martha Ross.

Fig. 90. Sometimes this shape appears in regular satin, rather than mother-of-pearl. Courtesy of Rose Colored Glass.

Fig. 91. This shape is most often found without a matching underplate. Collection of Stu Horn.

Fig. 92. Note how each swirls in a different direction. Attributed to Mt. Washington. Author's collection.

Fig. 94. This is, perhaps, a better shot of the smaller swirl mother-of-pearl satin rose bowl. Author's collection.

Fig. 93. Here's the same design on an unusual pedestal base. Attributed to Mt. Washington. Photo by Bill Pitt, courtesy of Brookside Antiques.

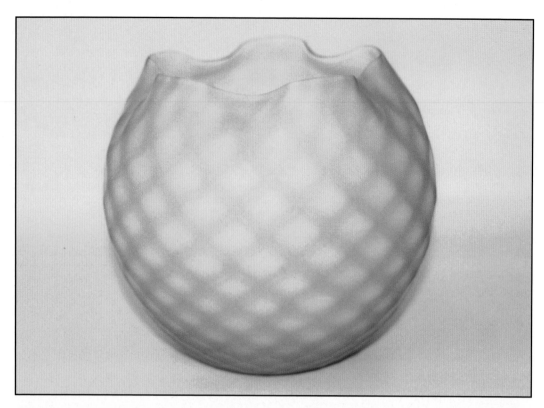

Fig. 95. As with regular satin, you don't find lavender cut velvet too often. Collection of Martha Ross.

Fig. 96. Cut velvet is a variation of mother-of-pearl satin in which the design is raised. Mt. Washington had a patent on this technique. Photo by Bill Pitt, courtesy of Brookside Antiques.

Fig. 97. Blue is probably the most common color in cut velvet rose bowls. As with regular mother-of-pearl, diamond quilted is also the most common pattern. Collection of Stu Horn. Photo by Stu Horn.

Fig. 98. This is an unusual pattern in cut velvet, and is probably Mt. Washington. Collection of Stu Horn.

Fig. 99. This cut velvet example looks as if the pattern wasn't raised enough to get the proper effect. The shape suggests Mt. Washington. Author's collection.

Fig. 100. Green satin Stevens & Williams with box pleat. Collection of Ruth Sparks.

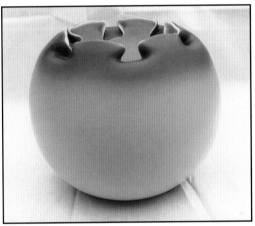

Fig. 101. Stevens & Williams of England had a patent on the box pleat, a square form of crimping. Author's collection.

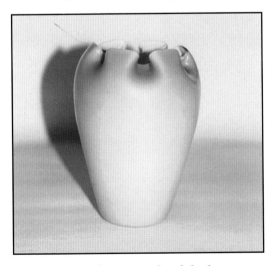

Fig. 102. Another example of the box pleat, this one on a tall blue piece which could also be considered simply a vase. Since the top turns in and not up or back out, it meets the definition of a rose bowl. Collection of Ruth Sparks.

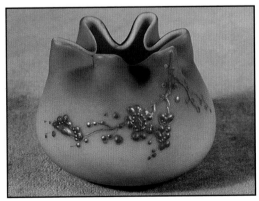

Fig. 103. Thomas Webb & Sons did rose bowls in some unusual shapes. Note the unusual color and blue interior. Photo by Bill Pitt, courtesy of Brookside Antiques.

Fig. 104. *Rare hobnail mother-of-pearl satin rose bowl. Collection of Ruth Sparks.*

Fig. 105. *Apricot Stevens & Williams Pompeiian Swirl. Photo by Bill Pitt, courtesy of Brookside Antiques.*

Fig. 106. *Stevens & Williams with box pleat. Collection of Martha Ross.*

Fig. 107. Stevens & Williams had a very interesting repertoire of colors. Photo by Bill Pitt, courtesy of Brookside Antiques.

Left: Fig. 108. Rich pink Stevens & Williams Pompeiian Swirl with box pleat. Photo by Bill Pitt, courtesy of Brookside Antiques.

Fig. 109. Stevens & Williams Pompeiian Swirl. Photo by Bill Pitt, courtesy of Brookside Antiques.

Fig. 110. Pompeiian Swirl in a typical Stevens & Williams heart shape. Photo by Bill Pitt, courtesy of Brookside Antiques.

Fig. 111. Pompeiian Swirl. Note the shape, crimp style, and blue interior. Photo by Bill Pitt, courtesy of Brookside Antiques.

Fig. 112. Stevens & Williams basketweave in brown satin glass. Photo by Bill Pitt, courtesy of Brookside Antiques.

Fig. 113. Blue Stevens & Williams basketweave. Photo by Bill Pitt, courtesy of Brookside Antiques.

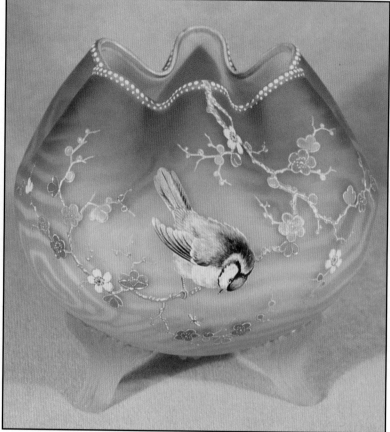

Fig. 115. Bohemian, footed, apricot satin, moire mother-of-pearl with bird decoration. Photo by Bill Pitt, courtesy of Brookside Antiques.

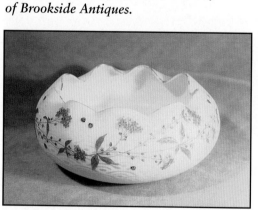

Fig. 114. Enameled squat white satin peacock eye mother-of-pearl. Note the lady bugs in the design. Photo by Bill Pitt, courtesy of Brookside Antiques.

Fig. 117. Bi-color "rainbow" mother-of-pearl on three toes. Note the prunt on the bottom. Photo by Bill Pitt, courtesy of Brookside Antiques.

Fig. 116. This Stevens & Williams blue satin air trap piece resembles the company's jewelled glass (see section 1.8.). Collection of Ruth Sparks.

Fig. 118. Unusual arched pattern of mother-of-pearl satin in Mt. Washington's Alice Blue color. Author's collection.

Right: Fig. 119. Thomas Webb blue diamond quilted mother-of-pearl with white cameo, said to once have belonged to author Albert Christian Revi. Collection of Stu Horn.

Above: Fig. 120. Rare gilded ribbed satin by Smith Brothers, purchased from the Smith family. Collection of Louis O. St. Aubin, Jr.

1.2. Lusterless and White Satin

Both satin and mother-of-pearl satin glass were made in white, but it is one of the rarest rose bowl colors, which is part of the reason I put it in a separate section. The other reason is that Mt. Washington, one of the two major producers of white satin, did not call it white satin, but instead called it "Lusterless." Created in 1881, and designed to resemble alabaster, Lusterless was one of the first types of art glass produced by Mt. Washington. They come in sizes ranging from 2-3/4 inches on up (5 inches is the most common).

Lusterless rose bowls are found in abundance in both decorated and undecorated styles. Many companies sold their blanks to be decorated by other firms, and apparently Mt. Washington sold Lusterless blanks in large quantities to the so-called cottage industry. Cottage decorators, many of whom are said to have worked in homes or cottages, decorated the glass but did not fire the decorations for permanence. As a result, a good number of Lusterless rose bowls are found with decorations which have nearly completely worn off. No doubt some of the decorations were done later by amateurs. Once you know how to recognize an authentic Mt. Washington decoration, you can spot the later replacements. Mt. Washington designs used a variety of earth tones such as greens, browns, and shades of rose. A bright blue flower found on one of the smallest Lusterless rose bowls obviously is not factory done.

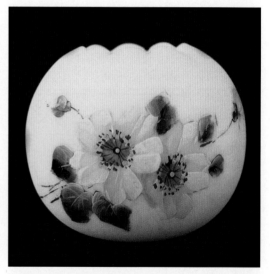

Fig. 121. Although the design is unfired, apparently it was done commercially, since it is frequently found on 5" Lusterless rose bowls. Author's collection.

Fig. 122. Lusterless is scarce in the 3-1/2" size. Author's collection.

Fig. 123. The blue flower indicates this design on this 2-3/4" mini was not done at the Mt. Washington factory. It was done commercially, however, since identical ones can be found. Author's collection.

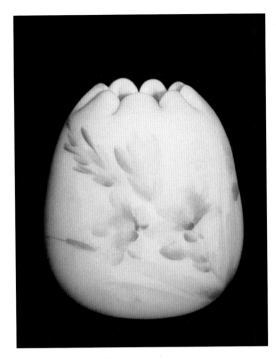

Fig. 124. Mt. Washington Lusterless rose bowls were done in the egg-style. Collection of Stu Horn.

Fig. 125. A Mt. Washington egg-style with a rare Cox Brownie design. Collection of Ruth Sparks.

Fig. 126. Another design done by the cottage industry. Photo courtesy of David and Irmgard Schmidt.

Mt. Washington Lusterless rose bowls are characterized by a softly rounded shape that is somewhat wider at the bottom than at the top, has nine crimps, and a perfectly round smooth concave pontil. The fact that signed Mt. Washington rose bowls exist in this shape provides proof that white satin rose bowls found in this shape are, indeed, a Mt. Washington product.

It is unknown just who made the other white satin rose bowls. The majority of them are found in a shape that is more spherical than their Mt. Washington counterparts. These have nine crimps that are much larger and bolder than those on Mt. Washington bowls. The most common size is 5-1/2 inches, but they are also found as small as 2-3/4 inches and as large as 10 inches. When found decorated, these bowls often have a band of heavy gold paint around the top. Pontils are usually ground smooth, but are sometimes found rough. I have never found a rough pontil on a Mt. Washington Lusterless rose bowl, however. Rose bowls identical in shape to these white satin ones were made in black amethyst, although these are considerably harder to find.

I have seen white herringbone mother-of-pearl satin rose bowls with colored interiors attributed to Mt. Washington, and off-white mother-of-pearl satin examples in the diamond-quilted pattern, which are by Webb. The origin of another shape in white diamond-quilted mother-of-pearl satin is still a mystery.

Fig. 128. This rose bowl is one of the few found in this shape with factory-applied enameling. This 3" example has a different floral design on each side. Collection of David Billings.

Fig. 127. The other white satin rose bowls found on the market are shaped like this one, which measures a whopping 7-1/2" tall. The cottage decoration is well done and intact. Author's collection.

Fig. 129. Second side.

Fig. 130. Third side.

Fig. 131. Fourth side.

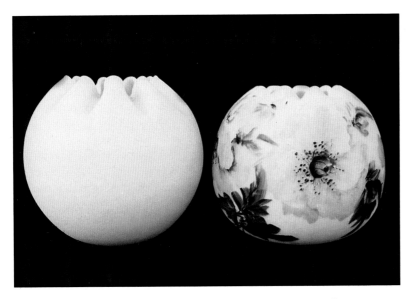

Fig. 132. Note the variation in shape between Mt. Washington Lusterless (right) and the other white satin. Author's collection.

Fig. 133. This worn cottage-decorated black amethyst example is shaped just like the white satins. 5" tall. Collection of Martha Ross.

Fig. 134. Note the difference in decorative style between Mt. Washington Lusterless (right) and the other white satin. Author's collection.

Fig. 135. Another variation in shape by an unknown maker. The cottage-decorated street scene is unusual. Author's collection.

1.3. Albertine and Crown Milano

In a marketing maneuver, Mt. Washington changed the name of its Albertine line to Crown Milano because the line wasn't successful under the previous name. By either name, the line is generally characterized by elaborate decorations with heavy gold accents. But, in the case of rose bowls, the colors and decorations on Crown Milano and Albertine are so soft and delicate that some might have a hard time associating them with the Crown Milano line.

Unlike their cousins in other shapes, Crown Milano and Albertine rose bowls have little, if any, gold, and the designs are fairly simple. Despite the contradiction in styles, some of these simply decorated rose bowls are found signed "Crown Milano." Others match the decorations found on signed pieces in other shapes.

Often, Albertine and Crown Milano rose bowls have Burmese coloring. Unlike Burmese glass, though, which gets its two-tone coloring from chemicals in the glass formula and the heat, Burmese-colored glass is simply painted or otherwise colored to look like Burmese. These Mt. Washington product lines are not the only ones to have Burmese coloring, but most Burmese-colored rose bowls are Mt. Washington.

Some Albertine and Crown Milano pieces were signed with a shape number written on the bottom in purple ink. The numbers found on rose bowls and their corresponding sizes are as follows:

620 —2-1/2 inches
619—3-1/2 inches
618—4 inches
617—5 inches
616—6-1/2 inches

Be aware, however, that the existence of a shape number on the bottom does not guarantee that the rose bowl is Crown Milano. These shape numbers were used on many Mt. Washington lines. The shape number "616," for example, could be found on a 6-1/2 inch Royal Flemish rose bowl in the same shape as the ones found in Crown Milano. You must consider all characteristics of the glass to determine if it is or is not Crown Milano.

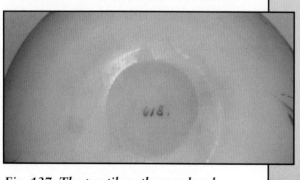

Fig. 136. Mt. Washington Albertine or Crown Milano rose bowl with an orchid design. Author's collection.

Fig. 137. The pontil on the rose bowl with the orchid decoration. Note that it is a perfect indented circle. 618 is the shape number.

Fig. 138. The back of the rose bowl.

Fig. 139. Another view of bowl in fig. 140.

Left: Fig. 140. This one does not have the Crown Milano mark, but other shapes in this design are signed. Author's collection.

Fig. 141. Third view of bowl in fig. 140.

Right: Fig. 142. This 2-3/4" Crown Milano exhibits the Burmese coloring for which the line is famous. Author's collection.

Fig. 143. Another Crown Milano in a
miniature 2-1/2" size. Author's collection.

Right: Fig. 144. This miniature Crown
Milano rose bowl still has the original
paper label. Collection of Ruth Sparks.

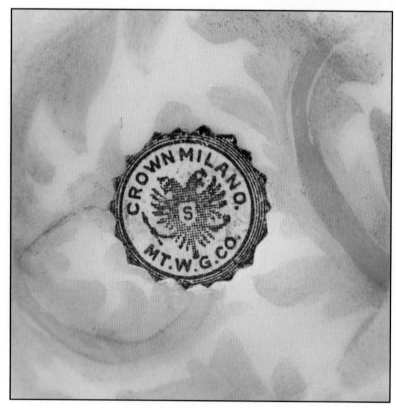

Fig. 145. A Crown Milano signature.

Fig. 146. A Crown Milano paper label.

Fig. 147. Mt. Washington Crown Milano.
Collection of Ruth Sparks.

Fig. 148. Mt. Washington Crown Milano Rose Bowl. Photo courtesy of David and Irmgard Schmidt.

Fig. 149. Mt. Washington Crown Milano. Note the softly colored roses. Photo by Bill Pitt, courtesy of Brookside Antiques.

Fig. 150. Mt. Washington Crown Milano Rose Bowl. Photo by Bill Pitt, courtesy of Brookside Antiques.

Fig. 151. Mt. Washington Crown Milano Rose Bowl. Photo by Bill Pitt, courtesy of Brookside Antiques.

Fig. 152. The decoration on this Crown Milano rose bowl features a rare mosaic floral. Photo by Bill Pitt, courtesy of Brookside Antiques.

Fig. 153. This undecorated yellow rose bowl is obviously Mt. Washington, due to the shape, crimp style, and appearance of the pontil. It was probably a Crown Milano blank that was never decorated, or a second. Collection of David Billings.

1.4. Burmese

First patented in 1885 by Frederick P. Shirley for the Mt. Washington Glass Co., Burmese is a single-layered opaque glass, shading from rose at the top to yellow at the bottom. The color was achieved by using small amounts of uranium oxide, gold, feldspar, and fluorspar, which turned the glass a sulphur-yellow color. Reheating the top portion of the glass turned it a delicate rosy pink.

I've read two stories in old antiques magazines about how Shirley invented this glassware, and both stories claim it was by accident. One says that Shirley was testing some opaque yellow glass and the ingredients for a batch of rose amber (Mt. Washington's amberina) were somehow dumped into the pot of yellow. Another relates that Shirley was working on a pot of yellow glass when he accidentally dropped his wedding ring into the batch! I have seen no verifiable confirmation for either story. But, the second account sure is the more interesting of the two! (If it is true, I wonder if he got in trouble with his wife.)

Fig. 154. Thomas Webb did make glossy Burmese, though examples are scarce. The egg shape also makes this miniature unusual. Photo by Bill Pitt, courtesy of Brookside Antiques.

Shirley presented several pieces to Queen Victoria and her daughter, Beatrice. Folklore says Queen Victoria was so enthralled with the glass that she exclaimed it reminded her of a Burmese sunset, hence the name. However, the more likely story is that it was so named simply because of the popularity of Oriental names at the time.

Queen Victoria commissioned Shirley to make more Burmese glass for her. Unfortunately for Her Majesty, Mt. Washington did not make rose bowls in its Burmese glass for her—or for anyone else, for that matter.

Fig. 155. This decoration, known as Prunus, is the one most often found on Thomas Webb Burmese rose bowls. 2-1/8" high. Author's collection.

Fig. 156. The shape of this miniature Burmese makes it extra special. Photo by Bill Pitt, courtesy of Brookside Antiques.

Fig. 157. *Note the glossy finish on this one, too. Photo by Bill Pitt, courtesy of Brookside Antiques.*

Fig. 158. *Decorated Webb Burmese miniature. Collection of Ruth Sparks.*

Fig. 159. *Note the butterflies on this miniature. Collection of Ruth Sparks.*

Fig. 160. *This one has an unusual decoration. 3-1/4" high. Photo courtesy of Stu Horn.*

Fig. 161. *Mt. Washington didn't make Burmese rose bowls in the classic style; however, this shape still meets the definition. The honeycomb pattern is rare. This shape is also found in amberina. 8" tall. Photo by Bill Pitt, courtesy of Brookside Antiques.*

A year after Mt. Washington got its patent, Thomas Webb & Sons acquired a license to make Burmese glass in England. Webb made rose bowls in sizes ranging from 2 inches to 3 inches in height. Some are undecorated, while others were hand painted at the factory and fired for permanence.

Burmese rose bowls have been reproduced. For information on the reproductions and how to tell the difference, see sections 3.2 and 3.6.

1.5. Peachblow

It all started with a Chinese porcelain vase and an auction. The "Peach Blow" vase, belonging to Mary Morgan, sold for $18,000 at auction on March 8, 1886, thus beginning the peachblow craze. Suddenly peachblow was the color of the day—as well as the topic of much satire.

The term "peachblow" is seen both as one word and as two, and it is sometimes capitalized and sometimes not. For the purposes of this book, it will be written as a lowercase single word—"peachblow"—unless a particular company's spelling is being used.

To collectors of Victorian art glass, the term "peachblow" refers to three distinct types of glass:

• "Wheeling peachblow," so nicknamed because it was made by Hobbs, Brockunier & Co., of Wheeling West Virginia. Originally marketed under the name "Coral," it shades from a deep, brick red at the top to a golden yellow at the bottom. It was produced in both glossy and matte finishes, and always has a creamy white lining.

• Mt. Washington peachblow was not nearly as well received as the Hobbs line, and was produced only from 1886 to 1888, making it the rarest form of peachblow today. Originally called "Peach Blow" or "Peach Skin," Mt. Washington peachblow shades from rose pink at the top to a blue gray at the bottom. It was made in both glossy and matte finishes, but was seldom decorated and is never lined.

• New England peachblow was advertised and sold under the name "Wild Rose," but the factory name for the product was, in fact, "Peach Blow." It shades from rose pink at the top to white at the bottom. It is also never lined. Like the other types, it was produced in both matte and glossy finishes, though matte finishes predominate.

Anyone familiar with peachblow will know that Gundersen, successor to the Mt. Washington Glass Co., reproduced peachblow in the 1950s. Although the company was supposed to have used the original Mt. Washington formula, the end result more closely resembles the New England product. Though the rose color found on the top of Gundersen peachblow is similar in color to that found on Mt. Washington, the bottom color is more white than blue gray. Gundersen's colors are a bit darker and more opaque in appearance than those on original peachblow of either type. Regardless, Gunderson is highly collectible, despite its comparative lack of age.

Fig. 162. *The color on this Thomas Webb peachblow is similar to that found on Wheeling peachblow. 3" high. Author's collection.*

Fig. 163. *The back of the rose bowl in fig. 162.*

Fig. 164. This one and the one shown in fig. 162 illustrate the variation in color found on Thomas Webb peachblow. Author's collection.

Fig. 165. The pontils on Thomas Webb spherical rose bowls show a cross section of all layers of glass.

The peachblow craze was not limited to the United States. Firms in England and other parts of the world also produced "peachblow" lines in the 1880s. Many rose bowl collectors would like to see Thomas Webb & Sons peachblow regarded with the same high esteem accorded the types discussed above. Webb's product resembles Wheeling peachblow, being lined, and shading from a deep red to a lighter golden apricot. Webb peachblow is often a bit more red than Wheeling, which is somewhat orange in comparison. Plus, Webb's glassware is a bit lighter and more translucent than Wheeling peachblow.

You can expect to pay well for any type of peachblow, which is no doubt accounts for at least some of the confusion. Collectors, it seems, are hopeless optimists, always thinking maybe they've found a

Fig. 166. Example of glossy Webb peachblow. 2-1/4" high. Author's collection.

"sleeper." But when it comes to peachblow, you will probably go your entire collecting life without finding a sleeper, and even if you do, you can still bet it won't be cheap. Prices for any of the three major types of peachblow start at around $300 to $400, with many examples priced at $1,000 and up. Even a piece of Webb peachblow will cost several hundred dollars.

Webb peachblow is the most popular form of peachblow among rose bowl collectors, no doubt because the line includes spherical rose bowls. Mt. Washington made some squat crimped bowls in its peachblow, but these are probably considered finger bowls or simply bowls. You won't find Mt. Washington peachblow in shapes anything like the crimped rose bowls found in Crown Milano.

Hobbs and New England did make round bowls that turn in at the top as part of their peachblow lines, so if you consider such a piece without crimps to be a rose bowl, then you're in luck. You can have peachblow rose bowls. But if you find a crimped piece, don't

Fig. 167. Glossy egg-style Webb peachblow on toes. Collection of Ruth Sparks.

be fooled. Neither Hobbs nor New England made crimped peachblow rose bowls. Nor did Gundersen. These are very important points. Many people confuse pink satin glass with peachblow, and pink satin rose bowls are abundant. If you find what you think is a New England or Gundersen peachblow rose bowl, you probably have a piece of pink satin glass instead. Remember: New England and Gundersen peachblow are not lined. Pink satin, on the other hand, usually is.

"Usually" is the key word here. Some unlined pink satin glass does exist, the age and origin of which I have not yet determined. When in doubt, look closely at the color. Most unlined pink satin glass is pretty much all one color, rather than changing dramatically from pink to white. Some unlined pink satin glass will change from pink to white, however. If you look closely at these pieces, you'll see that many have just the hint of a white lining. New England peachblow, on the other hand, is the same color both inside and out.

Burmese glass is often mistaken for peachblow, but keep in mind that Burmese always shades from rose pink to yellow, no matter who made it. It may look peachy, but it is not peachblow.

Collectors should be aware that, in addition to the major types of peachblow, there are many lines by other companies that are called peachblow. Both Fenton and L.G. Wright, for instance, produced their own "Peach Blow" lines, consisting of cased pink and white glass. Fenton's was made in 1939, and then again from 1952, to 1956. Wright's dates to the 1940s and 1950s.

So, if a piece of Fenton or Wright is tagged "Peach Blow," it may be represented truthfully. The collector simply must realize that this does not mean the piece is Victorian peachblow made by Mt. Washington, Hobbs, and New England, or even by Webb. Another quick way to tell is by the price, which will probably be less than $100. Be aware that Fenton and Wright pieces can still be mislabeled. Just because you know it to be Fenton or Wright and just because it is labeled "peachblow" doesn't necessarily mean it is really Fenton or Wright Peach Blow. Many people will attach the name "Peach Blow" to anything pink or peach-colored.

Peachblow rose bowls have been reproduced. For in-depth information on the various reproductions and how to tell the difference, see sections 3.2 and 3.5.

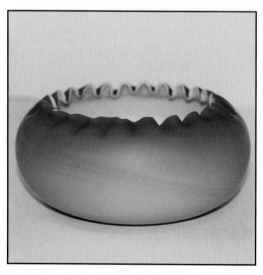

Fig. 168. The maker of this one is uncertain. It could be Webb or another English maker. Collection of Frank B. Strovel, Jr.

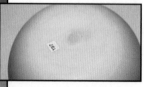

Fig. 169. World's Fair peachblow rose bowls come in various sizes, both decorated and undecorated, glossy and matte. Note the variations in shape and crimp style. Collection of Stu Horn. Photo by Stu Horn.

Fig. 170. World's Fair peachblow rose bowls have rough pontils. Pontils on New England peachblow pieces, though, would be ground smooth.

1.6. Spatter and Spangled Glass

Spatter glass is a multicolored ware in which small blotches or "spatters" of different colors are mixed together. Some people refer to this glass as "end-of-day," believing that glass factory workers routinely combined the remaining contents of several glass pots into one, and then made articles from it on their own time. While it's true that glassmakers did make pieces on their own time for their own use, or to trade for other things, spatter glass was manufactured in quantity for sale to the public.

Spatter glass rose bowls can be any color or combination of colors, and many consist of a layer of clear glass into which the colors are mixed.

The earliest known and attributable spatter glass rose bowls would be those made by Northwood in its Royal Ivy pattern. These don't have crimps, however. Spatter rose bowls with crimps come in both a tall shape and a more spherical configuration. Most of these are multicolored, though the actual colors may vary. The age and origin of these examples are unclear. Most seem to show proper wear for a piece of the Victorian era, yet it is also possible that some are more contemporary, being made by one of the companies along the Ohio River, possibly a company called Kanahwa. Regardless, they aren't the highest quality pieces, having visible seams and uneven crimping.

A variation of spatter glass is spangled glass. It contains flecks of mica, which looks a lot like glitter. The mica, found in both silver and gold, is sometimes arranged into a pattern; at other times it is found evenly scattered throughout the piece.

Fig. 171. Northwood's Royal Ivy pattern is one of the few attributable in spatter glass. Collection of Stu Horn.

Fig. 172. The origin of these rainbow spatter rose bowls is a mystery. However, I do believe they are Victorian, even if not of the highest quality. The pontils are rough and mold seams are visible. Collection of Stu Horn.

Fig. 173. At first glance, this looks like the same kind of glass as shown in fig. 172. But there's actually silver mica in this tall example.

Like its cousin, spangled glass can be any color or combination of colors, although yellow, apricot, and blue spangled rose bowls seem to be the most common. More rare colors include, green, red, tan, purple, and rainbow. Sometimes spangled rose bowls are decorated with enameling, and other times the inside layer of glass is colored, adding an interesting hue to the overall piece. Most spangled rose bowls are spherical with eight crimps, though some variations are also found.

The patent for spangled glass was first issued to Hobbs, Brockunier & Co. in William Leighton Jr.'s name. Another patent was issued that same year to the Vasa Murrhina Glass Co. The products of the two companies differ only slightly in the manufacturing process, and even in that respect not by that much. Spangled glass is frequently referred to as "Vasa Murrhina" because of the involvement of the Vasa Murrhina Glass Co. Spangled glass was also made in England and Bohemia, and it is difficult, if not impossible, to make accurate attributions.

Fenton reproduced a multicolored spangled glass in the 1960s, but it is not of much concern to rose bowl collectors since the company did not make rose bowls in this ware. For information on recent spangled glass rose bowls, see sections 3.2 and 3.4.

Fig. 174. Blue, yellow, and apricot are the most common colors in spangled rose bowls. Author's collection.

Right: Fig. 175. Spatter glass rose bowl basket with thorn handle. Collection of Ruth Sparks.

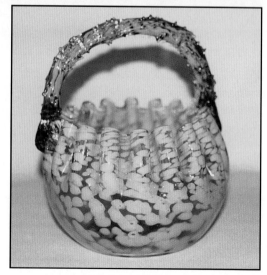

Fig. 176. Cranberry glass base with white spatter and silver mica. Nicely ground pontil. Also found in blue. Author's collection.

Left: Fig. 177. Pink spangled with applied toes and candy cane crimping. Probably English. Collection of Stu Horn.

Fig. 178. Rainbow spangle. Possibly Mt. Washington. Photo by Bill Pitt, courtesy of Brookside Antiques.

Fig. 179. Green spangled rose bowls are scarce. Photo by Bill Pitt, courtesy of Brookside Antiques.

Fig. 180. Purple spangled rose bowls are even more scarce than green, and more desirable. Collection of Ruth Sparks.

Fig. 181. This little basket-shaped rose bowl does have some mica in it, and a raised diamond quilted pattern in the glass. Collection of Phyllis Billings.

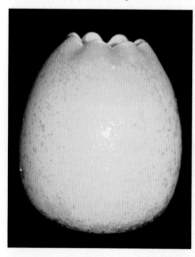

Fig. 182. An exceptional example with applied glass cherries. Photo by Bill Pitt, courtesy of Brookside Antiques.

Fig. 183. The spangled glass rose bowls were made in the egg style.

Fig. 184. Note the gorgeous green color and the diamond quilted pattern in the glass. Photo by Bill Pitt, courtesy of Brookside Antiques.

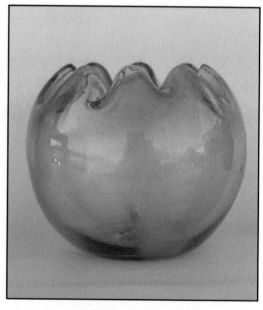

Fig. 185. This rose bowl has tiny flakes of mica, though they're hard to see. Its origin is unknown. Also found with pink stripes. Rough pontil. Author's collection.

1.7. Bohemian Glass

This area of Europe, now known as the Czech Republic, was and still is a major producer of rose bowls. Perhaps the most common type is the transparent rose bowl in various shades of green, ranging from a dark emerald to a light yellowish green, including some in what we call Vaseline (a transparent yellow-green glass which glows under ultra-violet black light due to uranium oxide content).

Many examples are decorated with gold or yellow-orange enameled scrollwork, with floral accents. The flowers are often made up of yellow and white enameled dots. Pontils vary from the very smooth and polished to completely rough.

The yellow-orange Bohemian enameling can be found on rose bowls made in other colors and in other types of glass. The Bohemians produced a number of souvenir satin rose bowls for the British Isles, for example, and these can be found enameled "A Present from London" or "A Present from Elgin." If you look closely, you might be able to see the words "MADE IN BOHEMIA" stamped on the bottom around the pontil on these bowls.

Fig. 186. A selection of "greenies," with all showing typical Bohemian-style enameling. Author's collection.

Some crystal and custard enameled rose bowls also hail from Bohemia. Just look for the telltale yellow-orange enameling, scrollwork, and dot enamel florals. Of course, not all Bohemian rose bowls have this color enameling. Some are decorated in other ways, including portrait decals or gilt. Likewise, yellow-orange enameling is not limited to Bohemian rose bowls. Consolidated's Shell & Seaweed pattern rose bowls are often elaborately decorated with yellow-orange enamel.

Rose bowls can be attributed to a few Bohemian firms, with one of the most famous being Moser. But beware! All that glitters is not Moser! Although Moser is famous for intricate enameled and gilded decorations, the fact is, many Bohemian firms made rose bowls in this style. Whenever a technique or style was popular, other companies copied it in order to nab a share of the market.

Fig. 187. Cranberry enameled toed rose bowl attributed to Moser, c. 1885. Author's collection.

Left: Fig. 188. Note the silver or platinum used in the decoration of this egg-shaped Moser rose bowl, c. 1885. 3" tall. Author's collection.

Fig. 189. This one has a somewhat unusual shape and four crimps. Collection of Frank B. Strovel, Jr.

Fig. 190. Another 4-crimper. This rose bowl is actually Vaseline opalescent. Author's collection.

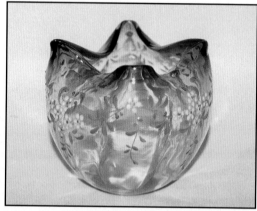

Fig. 191. Sometimes Vaseline Bohemian rose bowls can be found with different colored top rims. Severn collection. See also fig. 193.

Fig. 192. The jury is still out on whether this one is English or Bohemian. In many instances, decoration styles migrated from country to country. 2-1/2" high. Author's collection.

Fig. 193. The cranberry top edge makes this one unusual. The same exact design is found with a green edge. Collection of Stu Horn.

Fig. 194. Pontil on the bowl shown in fig. 196. Moser enameled only high quality blanks, always with polished pontils, like this one.

Fig. 195. Vaseline, with fine gold enameling, finely ribbed. 5" high. Author's collection.

Fig. 196. A smaller one in the same shape as fig. 197. Moser enameling, c. 1885. Author's collection.

Left: Fig. 197. Very large rose bowl, standing a good 12" tall. Attributed to Moser, c. 1885. Collection of Ruth Sparks.

Fig. 198. Solo shot of the larger intaglio Moser. Author's collection.

Fig. 199. Moser intaglio engraved on shaded amethyst. The larger one, which stands 2-7/8" tall, is signed Moser Karlsbad. Author's collection. The smaller one, which stands 2" high, has a slightly different shape. Collection of Stu Horn.

Fig. 200. Green shaded miniature Moser intaglio engraved. Rose bowl stands 2" high. Author's collection.

Right: Fig. 202. Trio of shaded gold glass enameled Siamese Moser bowls. Photo by Bill Pitt, courtesy of Brookside Antiques.

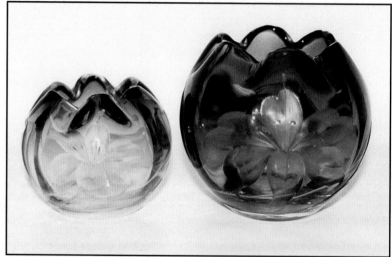

Fig. 201. Shot of amethyst and green Mosers, side by side. Author's collection.

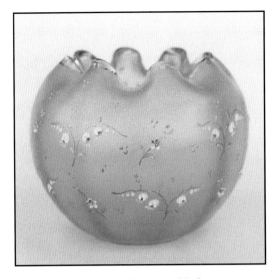

Fig. 203. Moser is the most likely source of this example, which features finely executed lily of the valley. But a definite attribution can't be made. Author's collection.

Fig. 204. The miniature blank was probably produced by the Meierhofen Moser factory outside of Karlsbad, Austria. Moser was responsible for the enameling. Collection of Ruth Sparks.

Fig. 205. The maker of this one is unknown. But, oh, what a gorgeous color! Photo courtesy of Larry and Kathy Murdie.

Fig. 206. It has a lot of gold and detailed floral enameling, but this style has not been confirmed as one Moser used. It is typical of other Bohemian glass houses, c. 1885. Collection of Martha Ross.

Left: Fig. 207. A number of Bohemian glass houses made this type of mottled glass. Collection of Martha Ross.

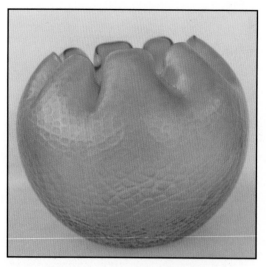

Fig. 208. This rose bowl is like Fig. 207, except it has an unusual yellow shading. These are also found in pink and green.

Fig. 209. No matter who produced it, lavender opalescent is not common. Author's collection.

Fig. 210. Note the similarities in enamel style to fig. 209. Collection of Martha Ross.

That's not to say rose bowls can never be accurately attributed to Moser. Some of Moser's works are signed, and similar unsigned pieces can also be attributed by comparing the decoration, shape, pontil, crimp style, and feel and color of the glass. Beware, however, because forged signatures abound (see section 3.8).

It's also important to understand that Moser started out as a decorator and did not make the blanks until 1893. Even after starting the factory, Moser continued to decorate blanks made by others, and sold blanks to others who added their own decorations. This makes attribution tricky.

Some Moser rose bowls don't glitter at all. These would be the amethyst and green intaglio engraved styles made between 1900 and 1910. These rose bowls range in size about 2 inches tall to 5 inches or more. They come in a couple of shape variations, with some being generally spherical with traditional crimping (typically six crimps) and others being straighter with more of a scalloped than a crimped top. Many of these are signed "Moser Karlsbad." Since not all are signed, it's important to note that another Bohemian firm, Harrach, also did intaglio cut work. The engraved rose bowls are found in two colors, amethyst and green. Moser did make other colors of shaded transparent glass, but thus far none of these have turned up in rose bowls. Some engraved rose bowls are found with enameled accents, but these are hard to find.

Fig. 211. Like the Moser examples, this one is decorated with scrollwork and tiny flowers, but the detail is not nearly as fine as those found on Moser bowls. Collection of Frank B. Strovel, Jr.

Fig. 212. The decoration is typical of Bohemian rose bowls, though this bowl could have been produced elsewhere. Author's collection.

Pay attention to the bottoms. Whether Moser made the glass or just decorated it, Moser pieces have a concave polished pontil or a smooth bottom (see fig. 194). If the pontil is rough, you can be sure the piece is someone else's work.

Loetz, another famous Bohemian firm, also produced a share of rose bowls. The most famous are iridescent, but it's important to understand that Harrach, Pallme-Koenig, and Rindskopf, among others, also made iridescent glass. Attributing these is difficult at best, and many which are not Loetz are mistakenly attributed to this firm. One thing you can count on is that Loetz rose bowls will not have rough pontils. If you find one with a rough pontil, it was made by someone else.

Another Bohemian technique that shows up frequently on rose bowls is applied-glass flowers, stems, and leaves. People like to think that if it has applied-glass flowers, it must be a Stevens & Williams piece, since this English firm is famous for its applied-glass Mat-Su-No-Ke flowers. However, details of applied-glass decorations weren't recorded in British pattern books because they were improvised as the craftsmen worked. Only the outlines of the glass shapes were recorded in pattern books, according to Charles R. Hajdamach in *British Glass: 1800-1914*. This makes them nearly impossible to attribute. Besides, the glass industry, like most industries, experienced changes from glassworkers moving from one company to another, and often one country to another.

The Bohemian firms of Harrach and Hosch made a number of pieces with applied glass flowers, particularly rose bowl baskets. These firms also did quality work, so it's important not to be too quick to attribute rose bowls with applied glass flowers to Stevens & Williams.

Fig. 213. This one is similar to the one shown in fig. 195. Exact origin unknown. Courtesy of GlimmerGlass Antiques.

Fig. 214. The gold scrollwork on this miniature cranberry example is typical of Bohemian glass houses. Collection of Martha Ross.

Fig. 215. Loetz with typical threaded design. Collection of Stu Horn.

Fig. 216. Rose bowls with this type of threaded design are often mistaken for Loetz, but are more likely Pallme-Koenig. Collection of Martha Ross.

Fig. 217. Pair of egg-style bowls decorated with cherubs. Marked "Austria." Collection of Martha Ross.

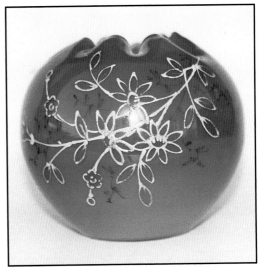

Fig. 218. This one looks remarkably like the "Bohemian" rose bowl offered as a premium for a new subscription to The Youth's Companion in 1896. Author's collection.

Fig. 219. The texture of this bowl causes many to assume it is Loetz. I believe it to be Bohemian, but not necessarily Loetz. Collection of Ruth Sparks.

Fig. 220. All that has applied glass flowers is not Stevens & Williams. The Bohemians made plenty of rose bowls with applied flowers, too. Collection of Stu Horn.

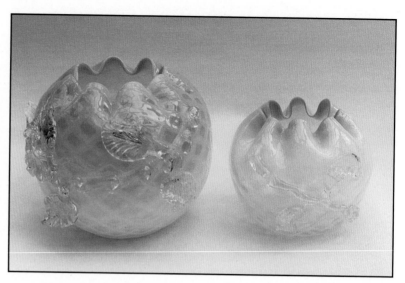

Fig. 222. The color combination on these is quite appealing, as is the diamond quilted pattern on the one on the left. Photo courtesy of Stu Horn.

Fig. 221. The Bohemians made quite a few rose bowl baskets. Photo by Bill Pitt, courtesy of Brookside Antiques.

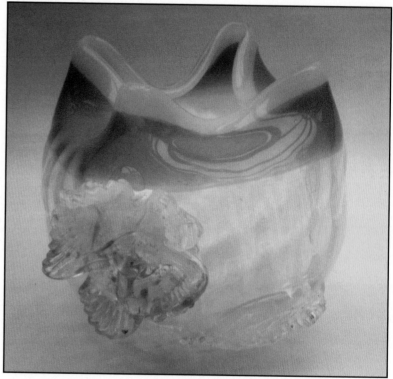

Fig. 223. The four-crimped shape leads me to believe this one is Bohemian. The flower also does not look English. The blue rim is quite interesting. Photo courtesy of Stu Horn.

1.8. Threaded Glass

Rose bowls were made in a number of threaded glass forms, primarily by Stevens & Williams. This British firm gave the name "jewelled glass" to a line of transparent threaded glassware that was patented in September 1886. Most Americans refer to it as "Jewell Glass." As with mother-of-pearl satin, the threaded designs are made by trapped air—only in this case the threading is done with a machine patented by the company. Pieces with vertical rows of small horizontal ribs came first, and were given the registry number 55693, which is etched on the polished pontil. Collectors today often refer to this as the "Zipper" pattern, though I could find no evidence that this name was ever used by Stevens & Williams.

A variation of the jewelled technique consists of a finely ribbed body with ovals spaced evenly between those in a raindrop effect. These items were given the registry number 81051. Rose bowls in both patterns are found in cranberry (which was referred to as ruby), crystal, green, sapphire blue, and amber. I've seen apricot- or tangerine-colored jewelled glass in other shapes and patterns, but, to date, never in rose bowls.

Jewelled glass rose bowls were made in both 2-1/4 inch miniatures and 4-inch versions. The miniatures have twelve tiny crimps, while the larger ones usually have six box pleats. On occasion, some of the larger rose bowls can be found with sixteen tiny crimps that match those on the miniatures. Squat and taller versions were also made, as was an unusual heart shape. By far, most of these are in the Zipper rather than the Raindrop pattern.

Osiris is a Stevens & Williams threaded glass which is not as well known in this country because of its relative scarcity, at least compared to jewelled glass. While working as artistic director for Stevens & Williams, John Northwood invented a number of new machines, including one that would create patterns as it pulled the threads. The machine was patented in February 1885, but Osiris glass did not show up in the line for another year, with full production beginning in 1887. Examples are usually marked "PATENT."

Fig. 225. Blue miniature Stevens & Williams "Zipper" pattern jewelled glass rose bowl, marked "Rd 55693." It stands 2-1/4" high. Author's collection.

Fig. 224. Miniature cranberry Zipper. Author's collection.

A number of sizes and colors of rose bowls were made in Osiris glass, often with interior colors other than white. Rose bowls in particular were given fancy crimps on other machines invented by Northwood. Some Osiris glass is even found with an airtrap or mother-of-pearl design.

Some other threaded glass rose bowls are out there, but attributing them is difficult at best. Two possibilities exist: One is Boston and Sandwich, and the other is Mt. Washington. So far, however, I have not been able to determine which is which. Certainly, Boston and Sandwich is better known for this treatment, but that doesn't necessarily mean that threaded rose bowls are Boston and Sandwich products.

Fig. 226. Miniature green Zipper.
Author's collection.

Fig. 227. Miniature crystal Zipper.
Author's collection.

Fig. 229. Cranberry miniature raindrop
pattern. Photo courtesy of Stu Horn.

Fig. 228. Miniature blue Stevens & Williams raindrop pattern
jewelled glass rose bowl. Marked Rd 81051. 2-1/4" high.
Author's collection.

Fig. 230. This was the first miniature rose bowl I ever bought. I didn't know at the time that it was Stevens & Williams jewelled glass.

Fig. 231. This larger Zipper is lighter in color than the miniature. Marked "Rd 55693." 4" high. Author's collection.

Fig. 232. Crystal miniature jewelled glass rose bowl in raindrop pattern. Author's collection.

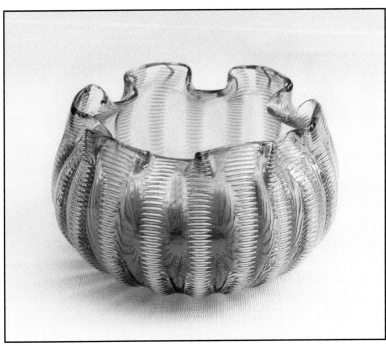

Fig. 233. Squat cranberry Zipper with box pleat. Photo courtesy of Stu Horn.

Left: Fig. 234. Stevens & Williams jewelled glass is one of the few types of glass which is just as stunning in crystal as in color. Author's collection.

Fig. 235. Heart-shaped cranberry Stevens & Williams raindrop pattern jewelled glass. 5" high. Marked "Rd 81051." Collection of Stu Horn.

Fig. 236. Cranberry threaded rose bowls, possibly by Mt. Washington or Boston & Sandwich. Collection of Stu Horn.

Fig. 239. Stevens & Williams Osiris glass with peacock eye mother-of-pearl design. Photo by Bill Pitt, courtesy of Brookside Antiques.

Fig. 237. The cranberry glass and amber threading make an interesting combination. Collection of Martha Ross.

Right: Fig. 238. Unusual Osiris rose bowl with a raised herringbone design. Photo by Bill Pitt, courtesy of Brookside Antiques.

1.9. Opalescent Glass

By adding bone ash to the batch and then reheating the piece, manufacturers were able to achieve an effect known as opalescence. Found most often in white, blue, green, canary/Vaseline, and cranberry, opalescent glass is transparent with milky highlights.

Pressed opalescent rose bowls appear in dozens of different patterns, some of which stand on toes or on pedestal bases. It seems the vast majority of pressed opalescent rose bowls were made by Northwood/Dugan, but a few were made by other companies such as Fenton.

Following is a list of pressed Victorian opalescent patterns known to include rose bowls, along with their makers. The first date of manufacture, when available, is listed following the pattern name. Since I cannot illustrate every one, I suggest studying a good book on opalescent glass patterns and familiarizing yourself with the patterns listed below.

BUCKEYE: Reverse Swirl, c. 1888, white, blue, and canary. Also made by Model Flint. Daisy & Fern, c. 1888, white, blue, green, cran. opal. Also made by North. & Jeff.

FENTON: Beaded Moon and Stars, c. 1907, white, blue, green, crystal. Beaded Stars and Swag, c. 1907, white, blue, green, and crystal.

HOBBS: Seaweed, c. 1890, not crimped, rare, white.

JEFFERSON: Coin Spot, white, blue, green, cranberry, copied by Fenton. (Note shape differences to tell old from new (see Chapter 3). Interior Swirl, blue, white, canary. Shell and Dots/Beaded Fans, c. 1895, blue, white, green.

MODEL FLINT: Wreath & Shell, c. 1900, blue, white, canary, crystal, decorated crystal, gilded.

NORTHWOOD/DUGAN: Beaded Cable, c. 1904, blue, green, white, canary. Beaded Drapes (may actually be Jefferson), c. 1905, green, white, Vaseline. Beaded Fleur de Lis, c. 1906, blue, green, white. Button Panels, c. 1902, white, blue, canary, rare in green or emerald. Cabbage Leaf, c. 1906, white, green, blue, canary. Cashews (whimsies). Daisy & Plume, c. 1907, green, white, and blue. Drapery, c. 1904, white and blue, often with gold edging. Fluted Scrolls aka "Jackson," c. 1898, white, blue, Vaseline, custard, green, and crystal. Finecut & Roses, white, blue, green. Also made by Jefferson. Inverted Fan & Feather (whimsies). Leaf and Beads, c. 1905, white, blue, green. Opal Open, c. 1899, white, green, blue, Canary. Pearls and Scales, c. 1905-1906, white, blue green, Vaseline, emerald. Pearl Flowers, blue green, white. Spanish Lace (originally called Opaline Brocade"), c. 1899, white, blue, cranberry. Reproduced by Fenton in cranberry. Vintage, blue, green, white.

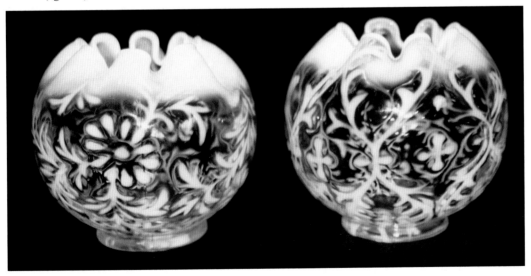

Fig. 240. People seem to have a tough time telling Daisy & Fern (left) from Spanish Lace (right). If it has flowers in it, it's Daisy & Fern. If it has + signs in it, it's Spanish Lace.

Fig. 241. The larger bowl is a late model by L.G. Wright. The smaller one could have been made by any number of companies. Also, see fig. 478. Photo courtesy of Stu Horn.

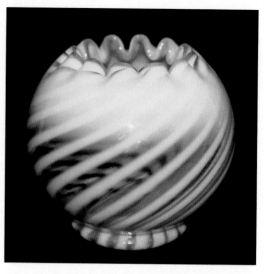

Fig. 242. Opalescent swirl pattern rose bowls with 12 crimps instead of 8 are attributed to Jefferson, based on old ads which show 12 crimps. Author's collection.

Fig. 243. Stevens & Williams Swirl opalescent is another you can identify, thanks to the box pleat. You don't see these often, though. Collection of Ruth Sparks.

Fig. 244. Virtually every company had an opalescent swirl pattern. It's difficult at best to tell one company's product from another. The frit on the rim of the blue one is typical of Northwood and Jefferson, however. Collection of Stu Horn.

Left: Fig. 245. Fancy Fantails was made by Northwood or Jefferson and is found in white, blue, green, and Vaseline. Collection of Stu Horn.

Fig. 246. Button Panels comes in white, blue, and canary, and is occasionally found in green and emerald. Collection of Ruth Sparks.

Fig. 247. Pearls and Scales is found in white, blue, green, Vaseline, and emerald. Collection of Ruth Sparks.

Fig. 248. Unlike its Carnival counterpart, which is found stemmed, opalescent Daisy and Plume is found only with three toes. It comes in green, white, and blue. Courtesy of Candace Reed.

Fig. 249. Shell and Dots and Beaded Fans are the same pattern, by Jefferson, except that Shell and Dots has dots on the base. They're hard to see, but they are on this piece. Collection of Martha Ross.

Fig. 251. *The maker of the Piasa Bird whimsy rose bowl is unknown. Found in blue and white, with other colors possible. Photo courtesy of Stu Horn.*

Fig. 250. *Northwood Beaded Drapes comes in white, green, blue, and Vaseline.*

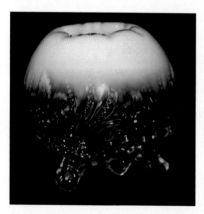

Fig. 254. *The origin of this lavender opalescent example is another mystery. Collection of Ruth Sparks.*

Fig. 252. *Better shot of white Piasa Bird.*

Fig. 253. *It's simple, but quite attractive. Unfortunately, its origin is also unknown. Author's collection.*

Some doubt exists over whether these patterns were made by Northwood or Jefferson. Fancy Fantails, c. 1905, white, blue, green, Vaseline. Fluted Bars and Beads, c. 1905-1906, white, blue, green, Vaseline, often with cranberry frit edging. Ruffles & Rings, c. 1906, blue, green, white. This one was originally produced by Jefferson, and then by Northwood.

UNKNOWN: Threaded Optic, blue. Dragon Lady (colors uncertain). Paneled Flowers, blue and white. Piasa Bird, white, blue. Woven Wonder, blue, white.

Stripe and Swirl patterns were also made in rose bowls by companies including Northwood, Nickel Plate, Jefferson, Beaumont, and English companies.

This list is as complete as possible, but it is important to note that rose bowls can be found in opalescent glass patterns not listed above.

In addition to pressed opalescent patterns, a number of blown and mold-blown opalescent rose bowls can be found, most of which incorporate some kind of vertical striping. The larger ones, measuring 3 inches to 5 inches in height, are found with applied glass flowers, and these are believed to be either English or Bohemian. These are found in crystal or frosted with white stripes alternating with blue, pink, or yellow.

Opalescent glass has continued to be produced right on through today. For more information on later opalescent rose bowls, see Chapters 2 and 3.

Fig. 255. It's also found with Coralene foliage. Collection of Ruth Sparks.

Fig. 257. Here is another mystery, found in blue opalescent, too. Similar bowls are sometimes found with applied foliage. Rough pontil. Author's collection.

Fig. 256. Rare opalescent pattern, believed to be of English origin. The blue to Vaseline color is also unusual. Photo courtesy of Stu Horn.

1.10. Custard

This opaque milky-yellowish glass resembles egg custard in color and glows under ultra-violet light. It is found in both pressed and blown rose bowls, though pressed patterns predominate. The pressed custard rose bowls are found in several patterns, and include: Fine Cut and Roses, Beaded Cable, Fluted Scrolls, Inverted Fan & Feather (All Northwood/Dugan), Ruffles and Rings (Northwood or Jefferson), and Persian Medallion (Fenton).

I have also found what I believe to be custard satin glass. (See fig. 24.) At first, other collectors and I called this color a pale green because an almost fluorescent green hue could be seen in the bottom near the pontil. However, after finding satin glass rose bowls in true green, I concluded these are more accurately described as custard. These are found undeco-rated as well as enameled and painted, and I believe most to be Bohemian in origin because of the yellow-orange enameling so typical of Bohemian glass. Of course, as discussed be-fore, not all yellow-orange enameling is Bohemian, but at this point, the Bohemian connec-tion is all I have to go on.

Glossy blown rose bowls are also found, many with applied glass flowers or fruit on them. Many people mistakenly believe them all to be made by Stevens & Williams. As discussed earlier, it's just as likely they are not. One thing you can check, though, is the pontil. Stevens & Williams would not have left a rough pontil.

Fig. 258. Fine Cut and Roses is found in Carnival, opalescent, and custard glass. Collection of Stu Horn.

Fig. 259. Although this looks more like a goblet than a rose bowl, most rose bowl collectors accept it as a rose bowl. Besides, the crimps would make drinking from it tough! Courtesy of Ar-Jo Antiques/Horatio Antiques.

1.11. Li'l Guys

Miniature rose bowls were made in many of the types of glassware already discussed, but I still felt they deserved to be discussed on their own. Some collectors are so passionate about the miniatures that they even requested that this book devote a full section to miniatures! Besides, some miniatures have no known larger-size counterparts.

When I first began collecting rose bowls, I thought that about 3 inches was as small as they got. Most people seem to be under the same misconception, since I see many 3-inch rose bowls described as "miniature" when they are really average sized. There is no real cut-off point at which a rose bowl goes from average-sized to miniature, but it is important to note that rose bowls are found measuring as little as 1 inch in height and diameter. Sit one of these babies next to a 3-inch version and there is no comparison!

Typically, miniature rose bowls measure between 2 inches and 2.5 inches in height/diameter. It doesn't sound like much of a difference, but these bowls are actually considerably smaller than their 3-inch counterparts. Interestingly, most of the miniatures were made in England and Europe—I'm not sure why. Perhaps there is no real reason—it may have just happened this way.

That's not to say American glass companies never made miniatures. Miniature rose bowls are found in pattern glass and in Mt. Washington's Lusterless and Crown Milano lines. Fenton made miniatures in both opalescent hobnail and Burmese.

The very tiny 1-inch rose bowls are definitely hard to find. I have seen exactly four. One was a Hawkes amethyst intaglio shaded cut-to-clear, which to this day I wish I had bought. The next was a tiny Daum Nancy, with a tree scene on it. But that one didn't speak to me in nearly the same way the Hawkes example did. Finally, I had the opportunity to privately purchase two tinies. These two, one in red and one in blue, were a wee bit bigger than the Hawkes and Daum pieces, and I have no idea who made them or how old they are. But I am glad I bought them, since I have not seen any that small since then.

Fig. 260. These are the tinies that I finally managed to acquire. The red one stands 1-3/8" tall and the blue, 1-1/4" tall.

Because of their exceptionally small size, I wondered if they were supposed to be salts. The seller, a private collector, said she believes they were intended to be cabinet pieces. I have had others insist they are salts. I've had still others insist they are rose bowls and not salts. Whatever you call them, they fit nicely into a rose bowl collection.

Fig. 261. Red tiny. 1-3/8" tall. Author's collection.

Fig. 262. Blue tiny. 1-1/4" tall. Author's collection.

This leads to another question. What exactly was a miniature rose bowl really supposed to be? By definition in most references, an ivy bowl or violet bowl is essentially the same thing as a rose bowl, only smaller. However, just as I said in the introduction, manufacturers were terribly inconsistent with their names. Sometimes an "ivy bowl" or "violet bowl" was even larger than a "rose bowl" made by the same manufacturer. For simplicity's sake, I won't use the terms "ivy bowl" or "violet bowl" unless referring to the original manufacturer names.

Miniature rose bowls originated in the Victorian era just like their larger cousins. But they were made all during the twentieth century as well. Illustrations of miniatures will be found throughout this book.

It should also be noted that exceptionally large rose bowls, measuring as much as 12 inches across are also found. These are just as scarce as the 1-inch tinies, and collectors should be aware that they exist.

Fig. 263. Since amberina is a transparent glass, it is not found in mother-of-pearl satin. The correct term for this shading is mother-of-pearl satin with amberina coloring. Most miniatures in mother-of-pearl glass are English. Photo by Bill Pitt, courtesy of Brookside Antiques.

Fig. 264. Miniature diamond quilted mother-of-pearl satin with Coralene decoration. Probably English. Photo by Bill Pitt, courtesy of Brookside Antiques.

Fig. 265. This one has a wonderful plum color. English. Photo by Bill Pitt, courtesy of Brookside Antiques.

Fig. 266. The blue on this mini mother-of-pearl example has lovely shading. Photo by Bill Pitt, courtesy of Brookside Antiques.

Left: Fig. 267. Brown satin mother-of-pearl miniature. Photo by Bill Pitt, courtesy of Brookside Antiques.

Fig. 268. Most Webb rose bowls with Jules Barbe's prunus decoration are miniatures. Photo by Bill Pitt, courtesy of Brookside Antiques.

Fig. 269. Back of the bowl in fig. 268.

Fig. 270. Brown satin miniature, probably Webb. Photo by Bill Pitt, courtesy of Brookside Antiques.

Fig. 271. Most Webb Burmese rose bowls are miniatures. Collection of Stu Horn.

Fig. 272. The enameled dots on this Burmese miniature are unusual. Photo courtesy of Stu Horn.

Fig. 274. Although these are probably English, further details on their identities are not known. They are found in both frosted and unfrosted finishes in the colors shown, plus a blue and white stripe. 2-3/8" high. Polished concave pontils. Author's collection.

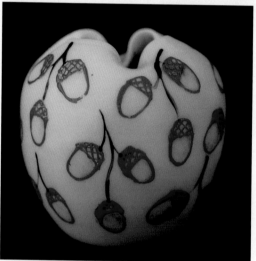

Fig. 273. Sometimes you feel like a nut . . . Author Cyril Manley attributes this shape to Webb, but no one who has seen this bowl can believe the decoration is really by Webb! Still, a cutie at 2-3/4" tall. Author's collection.

Fig. 275. These have the same basic shape and crimp style as the ones shown in fig. 214. But they have rough pontils. The pink one stands 2-1/8" tall. The blue one, 2-1/4". Author's collection.

Fig. 276. This miniature shape is also found with a satin finish. But it has a polished pontil. Collection of Martha Ross.

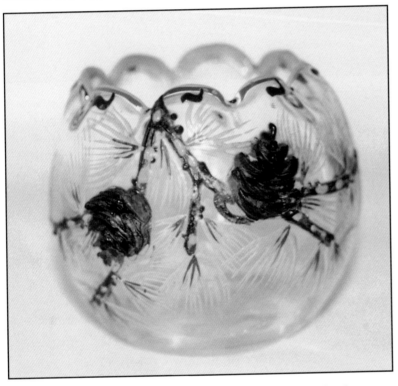

Fig. 278. Webb cameo miniature with 4 crimps. Collection of Ruth Sparks.

Fig. 277. The pine cones on this one are actually raised! About 2-1/4" high. Collection of Martha Ross.

Fig. 279. This shape and decorative technique has been attributed to Webb by British author Cyril Manley. 2-7/8" tall. Collection of Stu Horn.

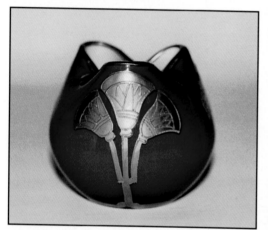

Fig. 281. Red rose bowls are very unusual. 2" high. Collection of Ruth Sparks.

Fig. 280. Same as fig. 279, except this has no feet. Private collection.

Fig. 282. Webb. Same shape as example in fig. 167. Collection of Ruth Sparks.

Fig. 283. Brown satin. These stand about 3" high. Collection of Ruth Sparks.

Fig. 284. Another Webb shape, this one in cranberry. Courtesy of Rose Colored Glass.

Fig. 285. Pink satin miniature, courtesy of GlimmerGlass Antiques.

Fig. 286. Apricot satin MOP, 2-1/2" high. Collection of Frank B. Strovel, Jr.

Fig. 287. *A miniature in the hard-to-find Flower and Acorn pattern of mother-of-pearl satin. Photo by Bill Pitt, courtesy of Brookside Antiques.*

Fig. 288. *Another Flower and Acorn MOP, this one in an unusual color. Photo by Bill Pitt, courtesy of Brookside Antiques.*

Fig. 289. *Both the style of enameling and the glass treatment suggest this one is Bohemian. 2" tall, ground pontil, glows under ultraviolet light. Also found with rubena verde coloring. Author's collection.*

Fig. 290. *Bohemian "greenies" can be found in all sizes. This one is 2-1/2" tall. Polished pontil. Author's collection.*

Fig. 291. This Murano-style is made like a hollow, crimped paperweight. 2-1/8" tall. Its age is unknown. Author's collection.

Fig. 292. On the opposite of the spectrum from miniatures are giant rose bowls, like this one in decorated blue satin. It stands a good 10" or 12" tall. Collection of Ruth Sparks.

Fig. 293. Although a definite attribution can't be made on this giant, it is no doubt of Bohemian origin. Collection of Ruth Sparks.

1.12. Pattern Glass

This section posed some interesting questions. First of all, extensive reference material already exists on pattern glass, and I don't want to repeat it. Second, since most pattern glass rose bowls are not crimped, they're not as popular with rose bowl collectors as other types. Still, pattern glass rose bowls are among the earliest documented (the earliest year I could find was 1880) and they're important from that standpoint.

In other sections, I have listed the maker first, and then the patterns by that maker. I'm going to do the opposite in this section, since most glass patterns were made by a number of companies. Following are the known patterns. I often find pattern glass rose bowls that I can't identify, so I am sure many more exist. This list is not all-inclusive, and others may have yet to be discovered.

ARTICHOKE: Fostoria (called it Line #205), c. 1891. Clear.

AUSTRIAN: Indiana Tumbler & Goblet Co. (Line #200), c. 1897; Federal, c. 1914; Indiana Glass Co., c. 1907. Canary, yellow, and clear.

BLOCK AND FAN: Richard & Hartley Glass Co., c. 1885; U.S. Glass Factory E, c. 1891. Clear.

BLOCK & LATTICE: Probably Crystal Glass Co., c. 1892. Clear.

BRITANNIC: McKee & Bros. Glass Works, 1894-1903. Clear and ruby stained.

CHAMPION: McKee, 1894-1917, also National Glass Co. Clear, ruby stained, amber stained.

CORONA: Greensburg Glass Co., c. 1894. Molds moved to National's McKee factory after merger. Clear.

DIAMOND BAR & BLOCK: O'Hara Glass Co., 1886-1892. Continued by U.S. Glass. Clear.

EUREKA: National Glass Co. at McKee factory, 1901-1904. Clear, ruby stained.

Fig. 294. Zippered Swirl and Diamond miniature made by U.S. Glass. It's found in clear, lustre, and ruby stained, c. 1895. 2-1/4" high. Author's collection.

Fig. 295. Zippered Swirl and Diamond in crystal. Collection of Martha Ross.

Fig. 296. The Roanoke pattern rose bowl originally came with a wire holder and chain so it could be hung. Made by Gillinder & Sons c. 1885 and U.S. Glass, c. 1891. Author's collection.

FOSTER BLOCK: Fostoria, c. 1888. Clear, ruby stained.

GALLOWAY: U.S. Glass, 1904-1919; Jefferson, 1900-1925. Clear and clear with rose.

HAWAIIAN LEI: J.B. Higbee Glass Co., 1900s. Clear.

HEART WITH THUMBPRINT: Tarentum Glass Co., 1898-1906. Clear, ruby stained.

HICKMAN: McKee, c. 1897. Clear, emerald green.

INVERTED STRAWBERRY: Cambridge Glass Co., 1912-1918. Clear.

KINGS 500: King Glass Co., c. 1891. Reissued by U.S. Glass, Factory K, 1891-1898. Clear, cobalt.

LATE BLOCK: George Duncan, c. 1890. Continued by U.S. Glass, Factory D. Clear.

MAJESTIC: McKee, 1893-1903, National Glass Co. Clear, ruby stained.

MARDI GRAS: George Duncan & Sons & Co., c. 1899; Duncan & Miller Glass Co., 1898 1920. Clear, ruby stained.

MINNESOTA: U.S. Glass, Factories F and G, c. 1898. Clear.

PANELED THISTLE: Higbee, 1910-1920; Jefferson, c. 1914. Clear.

PINEAPPLE & FAN #1: A.H. Heisey & Co., c. 1897. Clear, emerald green.

PINEAPPLE & FAN #2: Adams & Co., continued by U.S. Glass, c. 1891. Clear.

PRISCILLA: Dalzell, Gillmore & Leighton, 1880s, continued by National Glass Co., c. 1899. Clear.

PURITAN: Robinson Glass Co., c. 1894. Clear, ruby stained.

RED BLOCK: Bryce Bros., Central Glass Co., Doyle & Co., c. 1885; Fostoria c. 1890; George Duncan, Model Flint Glass Works, Pioneer Glass Works, c. 1897-1907. Ruby stained.

REVERSE 44: U.S. Glass, c. 1912. Clear, clear with gold or platinum.

ROANOKE: Ripley Glass Co., c. 1885. Reissued by U.S. Glass Factory F. Clear.

ROYAL IVY: Northwood, c. 1899. Clear frosted, rubena, frosted rubena (see fig. 332).

SCALLOPED SIX POINT: George Duncan, 1897-1912. Continued production by Duncan & Miller. Clear.

SNAIL: George Duncan, c. 1891. Reissued by U.S. Glass Factory D and later Factory P. Clear.

VICTORIA: Fostoria, c. 1890. Clear and clear frosted.

Fig. 297. Duncan Block rose bowls come in a variety of sizes, c. 1887. Courtesy of Odie and Joan Fincham, Jr.

Fig. 298. Tacoma pattern by Model Flint. Comes in four sizes: 3-1/2", 4-1/2", 5-1/2", and 6-1/2" in crystal, ruby stained, and amber stained. It was first introduced by the Greensburg Glass Co. (c. 1892-1898) and then the molds were transferred to Model Flint. Author's collection.

Fig. 299. The pattern name on this rose bowl is Banded Block. No previous references have identified a manufacturer. Author's collection.

Fig. 300. Majestic, which comes in both clear and ruby stained, was made by McKee & Bros. in Jeannette, PA, 1893-1903. Collection of Martha Ross.

Fig. 301. This cute little miniature is in the Puritan pattern by the Robinson Glass Co., c. 1894. Also found in ruby stained. Author's collection.

Fig. 302. Rose bowls are found in Duncan's Snail and Double Snail patterns, which the company considered one pattern, c. 1891. Also reissued by U.S. Glass. Collection of Stu Horn.

Fig. 303. The Victoria pattern by Fostoria is found both frosted and unfrosted, c. 1890. The bottom is marked "PAT'D." Author's collection.

Fig. 304. An outside view, showing what the rest of the bowl looks like.

Fig. 305. Rose bowls apparently were used for advertising. This one advertises Joseph Kuhn & Son clothing. Collection of Martha Ross.

Fig. 306. U.S. Glass Cube and Fan, also known as Pineapple and Fan. Courtesy of Odie and Joan Fincham.

Fig. 307. Thumbprint pattern. Courtesy of Odie and Joan Fincham.

Fig. 308. This also appears to be Cube and Fan, but with a patterned top. Collection of Martha Ross.

Fig. 309. The pattern on this one is unidentified. The top is etched "Isabella Saratoga 1897." Author's collection.

1.13. Miscellaneous Victorian Glass

Before moving on, I should mention that rose bowls were also made in cut glass. At first, I was ambitious enough to think I could cover them too, but that hasn't happened. Cut glass is a whole field in and of itself. Besides, cut glass rose bowls were not crimped, and would, therefore, not fit with the primary emphasis of this book. A few examples are shown, and collectors should be aware that they do exist. A number of good references will assist with pattern identification.

Rose bowls were made in a multitude of other types of glass, and even porcelain and pottery. It's not practical to attempt to cover them all in depth in this one volume. Examples of these varieties are shown in photos, with some information in the photo captions.

Fig. 310. Unusual cut glass rose bowl by the Smith Brothers and purchased from the Smith family. Collection of Louis O. St. Aubin, Jr.

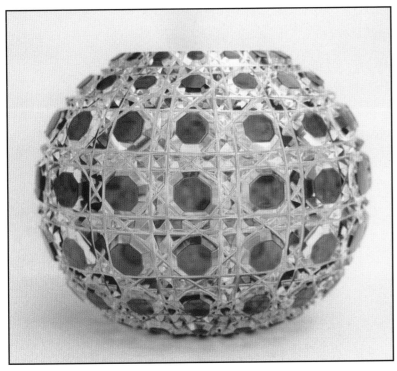

Fig. 311. Cut glass rose bowls are sometimes found cut to clear, as well as in just crystal. Collection of Frank B. Strovel, Jr.

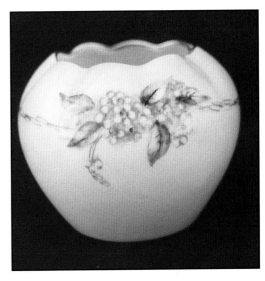

Fig. 312. Rose bowls are not limited to glass. This porcelain example, marked "O&EG Royal Austria" was made by Oscar & Edgar Guthers, Mfs, of Altrohlau, Bohemia, c. 1899-1918. For more information on non-glass rose bowls, see Chapter 2. Author's collection.

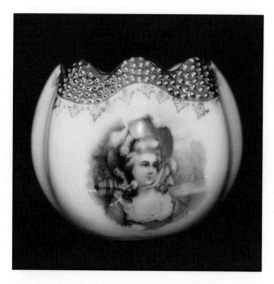

Fig. 313. This one is marked with the indented number 429 and another symbol which I can't make out. Although its origin and exact age can't be determined, the portrait suggests it is Victorian. The back says "Think of me" in gold Gothic lettering. 2-3/8" high. Author's collection.

Fig. 314. From a distance, this one looks like painted wood. But it is actually ceramic. It is marked "WS&S 2602." The initials stand for "W. Schiller & Sons," a Bohemian company. It dates from 1895. Courtesy of Andy Schilero.

Fig. 315. Stevens & Williams Mat-Su-No-Ke rose bowl. This Japanese-style technique is characterized by stylized applied glass flowers. They are sometimes marked "Rd 15353." Photo courtesy of Larry and Kathy Murdie.

Fig. 316. Another Mat-Su-No-Ke rose bowl example in a glossy finish. Mat-Su-No-Ke translated means "The Spirit of the Pine Tree"—even though the decorative technique has nothing to do with pine trees. Collection of Ruth Sparks.

Fig. 317. This beauty is pre-Nippon Japanese, c. 1880. Author's collection.

Fig. 318. Glossy red to pink color Mat-Su-No-Ke. This color resembles peachblow. Courtesy of Search Ends Here.

Fig. 319. Mat-Su-No-Ke rose bowls can be found in a number of shape variations. Collection of Ruth Sparks.

Fig. 320. These are identical in shape to the one shown in fig. 273. I can't imagine Webb decorating these, either! Collection of Ruth Sparks.

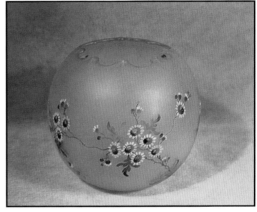

Fig. 321. Rare Mt. Washington Royal Flemish rose bowl. Note the unusual top. Photo by Bill Pitt, courtesy of Brookside Antiques.

Far Left: Fig. 322. The shape and quality of the glass on this one suggest it is Bohemian, but I am not sure. The enameled wisteria is nicely done. Author's collection.

Left: Fig. 323. This is about as close to Webb's style as any of these in this shape have come. Collection of Ruth Sparks.

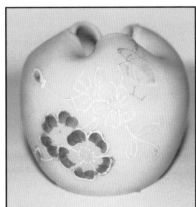

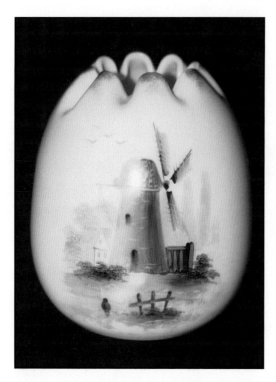

Fig. 324. Mt. Washington egg-shaped Delft Ware. Collection of Ruth Sparks.

Fig. 325. Don't confuse this with Stevens & Williams Zipper threaded glass. This is a copycat. It is found in pink, Caribbean blue, and this amber. Other colors possible. Rough pontil. Author's collection.

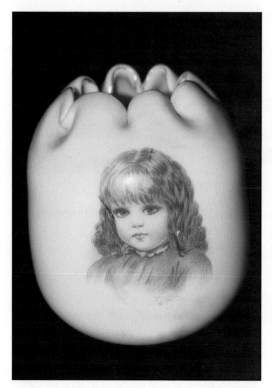

Fig. 326. This rose bowl features a charming portrait of a little girl. Collection of Ruth Sparks.

Fig. 327. This dark green rose bowl features a brown goddess and lion's head prunts on the side. Ground pontil. About 3" high. Photo courtesy of Larry and Kathy Murdie.

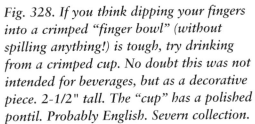

Fig. 328. If you think dipping your fingers into a crimped "finger bowl" (without spilling anything!) is tough, try drinking from a crimped cup. No doubt this was not intended for beverages, but as a decorative piece. 2-1/2" tall. The "cup" has a polished pontil. Probably English. Severn collection.

Fig. 329. Pink and white swirl rose bowl. Origin unknown. Collection of Stu Horn.

Fig. 330. Opaline rose bowl with unusual ring around the middle. Collection of Martha Ross.

Fig. 331. The Museum of American Glass at Wheaton Village has a rose bowl like this one, identified as having been made by Emil Stanger of the south Jersey area. Ground pontil. Author's collection.

Fig. 333. The origin of this one is a mystery. Note the fine diamond pattern in the glass. Rough pontil. Author's collection.

Fig. 332. Rubena is a cranberry to clear color, seen here in Northwood's Royal Ivy pattern. Collection of Stu Horn.

Fig. 334. Camphor glass is a cloudy glass which can also be colored. These two have tiny openings. Maker unknown. Collection of David Billings.

Fig. 335. Camphor glass example with cottage decorated scene. Collection of Martha Ross.

Fig. 336. Frosted white swirl, probably Stevens & Williams, due to crimp style. Polished pontil. Collection of Stu Horn.

Fig. 337. A number of companies did overshot glass, and attributions are difficult. Note the bright red flowers. Collection of Ruth Sparks.

Fig. 338. Cased Thomas Webb bowl with three toes. Photo courtesy of Stu Horn.

Fig. 339. Bottom of bowl.

Fig. 340. A child is an unusual decoration, and two children on one bowl is even more unusual. This piece appears to be Bohemian. Collection of Ruth Sparks.

Fig. 341. This rose bowl is very lightweight, almost like Bristol glass. Rough pontil. Collection of Ruth Sparks.

Fig. 342. This one no doubt came from the same place as the one shown in fig. 341. The weight of the glass, shape, pontil mark, and gold highlights are the same. Author's collection.

Fig. 343. Back of bowl in fig. 342.

Fig. 344. Custard bowl with enameled figures. It is not marked, but probably is of Austrian origin since others similar to this are found marked. 5-1/4" high. Rough pontil. Author's collection.

Fig. 345. Vaseline opalescent stripe, with applied glass flower. This style was made both in Bohemia and England. Collection of Martha Ross.

Fig. 346. This bi-colored one is not made of heat-sensitive glass. The color is painted on, probably to imitate peachblow. Collection of David Billings.

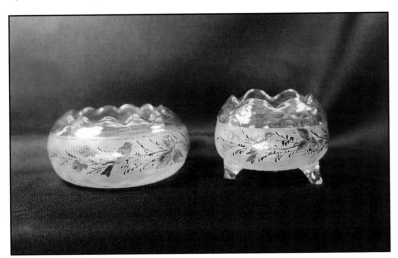

Fig. 348. "Mid West Pomona" was not made by New England and is usually associated with pressed copy cats. Still, these examples are quite attractive. Photo courtesy of Bob and Marjorie McCleskey.

Fig. 347. Pomona, made by the New England Glass Works, has an interesting history. The original patent, issued in 1885, called for the body to be covered with a wax or acid-resisting material and then a series of curved lines cut through the resist. This process was costly and time-consuming, so a less-expensive means, involving the use of an acid-resisting powder followed by an acid bath, created the frosted finish. The early means is now referred to as "First Grind" with the second process being "Second Grind." Since First Grind is rare, it's only natural that more rose bowls are found in Second Grind. This example is from the collection of Ruth Sparks.

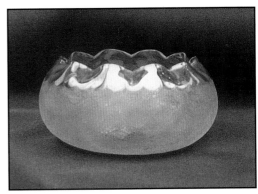

Fig. 349. A First Grind Pomona rose bowl. Photo courtesy of Bob and Marjorie McCleskey.

Fig. 350. Fancy blue bowl with applied
glass rim and feet. Collection of Stu Horn.

Fig. 351. Etched crystal with polished pontil. Author's collection.

Fig. 352. Cranberry rose bowl (thought by some to be a finger
bowl, see fig. 89) with underplate. Bowl has polished pontil.
Underplate has a 16-point star cut in the base. Author's collection.

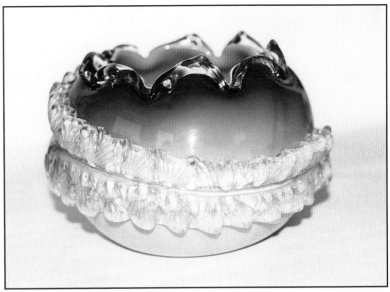

Fig. 354. *The acanthus leaf was a popular applied glass decoration made both in England and Bohemia. Collection of Ruth Sparks.*

Fig. 353. *Yellow hobnail rose bowl basket with applied crystal handle. Photo by Bill Pitt, courtesy of Brookside Antiques.*

Fig. 355. *This shape is more typical of Peloton rose bowls, which are usually miniatures. Photo by Bill Pitt, courtesy of Brookside Antiques.*

Fig. 356. *Peloton rose bowl without the foot. Photo by Bill Pitt, courtesy of Brookside Antiques.*

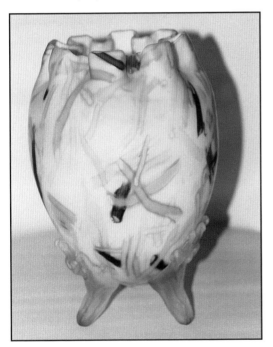

Fig. 357. *Peloton glass was patented first in Bohemia by Wilhelm Kralik, who was working for Harrach, and was later copied by English firms. Peloton is characterized by filaments of various colors in a base of clear, white, or colored glass. This shape is unusual for a Peloton rose bowl. Collection of Ruth Sparks.*

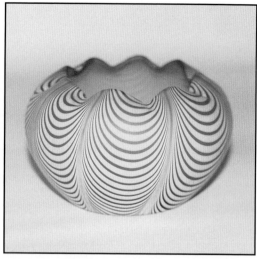

Fig. 358. Nailsea rose bowl. They're most often found in this squat shape. Collection of Ruth Sparks.

Left: Fig. 359. Lightweight Bristol-type glass bowl with unusual Indian decoration. Collection of Martha Ross.

Fig. 360. Low frosted bowl with Coralene. Photo courtesy of Stu Horn.

Fig. 361. Hobnail was around on rose bowls long before Fenton made it famous. Found in amber and probably other colors. Collection of Stu Horn.

Fig. 363. *This treatment is found in two sizes, though you seldom see the larger size. Photo courtesy of www.eapg.com.*

Fig. 362. *Grouping of rose bowls from Dugan's Japanese, Venetian, and Granite-ware lines. Ron Teal, Sr., author of* Albany Glass: Model Flint Glass Company of Albany, Indiana, *attributes the yellow one in the back to Model Flint, saying that shards for this treatment were found at that plant. So, apparently more than one company did this treatment. Author's and Stu Horn's collections.*

Fig. 364. *This shape is also found in solid colors. Photo courtesy of www.eapg.com.*

Fig. 365. *Close-up showing the Dugan (Model Flint?) Graniteware treatment, which was produced by rolling the gather into colored frit. Collection of Martha Ross.*

1.14. A Word About Decorations

Rose bowls are found with all kinds of decorations, from painted and enameled flowers to decals of portraits, cherubs, or buildings. These generally enhance the beauty of the glass, and hence its value, but collectors should be aware of certain pitfalls when purchasing decorated glassware.

In Victorian times, many glass companies sold undecorated blanks to companies that did nothing but apply decoration. As discussed in the section on white satin, such decorators are often referred to as the "cottage industry" because decoration was said to have been done in homes or cottages. Wherever it was done, cottage decorated pieces pose certain problems. Any time enamel, paint, or a decal is applied to glass, it must be fired for permanence. Since the average Joe doesn't have a glass furnace, it's pretty safe to assume that most amateur decorators, and even some professional cottage decorators, didn't fire their pieces to make the decorations permanent.

Fig. 366. Light green/custard colored rose bowl with factory applied re-fired enameling. Probably Bohemian. Collection of David Billings.

Eventually, those designs will fade, chip, or otherwise wear off. This is why it is very important for collectors to be able to distinguish between factory-applied fired decorations and non-permanent unfired ones.

Decals are complete pictures applied all at once, like an iron-on patch. Usually factory-applied, and permanent, decals generally depict something unusual such as cherubs, people, or buildings, although floral decals are used, too. You can spot a decal by looking for a lack of brush strokes—the design being made up of dots, or straight, thin lines instead.

Enameling, characterized by a slightly raised surface, is done at the factory and made permanent. After awhile, you'll start to see the same designs over and over again on rose bowls of different colors and sizes.

Painted designs differ from enameling in that they are more flat, having little height compared to enameling. Hand-painted designs were frequently applied after the rose bowl left the factory.

If you like hand-painted designs, though, take heart. Some were actually done at the factory. Webb's Burmese miniatures are a prime example, though other companies such as Mt. Washington and Fenton also fire hand-painted designs.

In order to determine if a rose bowl (or any piece of glass) has a cottage-done or unfired decoration, look closely at the design. You'll no doubt see at least a few spots where the paint has chipped or worn away. If the decoration is particularly old, the paint may look, well . . . old, and probably a little dirty or discolored. No matter how old, a factory-fired paint job will look new and bright.

If you own any cottage-decorated rose bowls, be sure to clean them cautiously. I have successfully used window cleaner, taking care not to spray directly onto the paint or to rub too hard.

Values for well-done, cottage-decorated rose bowls are comparable to prices for enameled ones. If the design is amateurish, chipped, worn, or faded, the decoration may actually detract from the value of the piece, rather than adding to it. The decoration is, after all, a statement about the overall quality of the piece.

Although enameled and factory-applied decorations are generally more desirable, don't completely dismiss cottage-decorated rose bowls. After all, each one does represent a unique piece of art history. But make purchases armed with knowledge and understanding about what exactly you're getting.

Fig. 367. Another example of factory applied enameled decorations, these done in gold. Probably Bohemian. Author's collection.

Fig. 368. Cottage (unfired) decoration. Note how the white on the petals has grayed and chipped in places. Author's collection.

Fig. 369. Cottage (unfired) decoration on mother-of-pearl satin. These were not done when the bowl was new, however. The mother-of-pearl is bruised and the paint is done over the bruises. Author's collection.

Fig. 370. More examples of cottage (unfired) decorations.

Fig. 371. This is what can happen to an unfired decoration over time. Author's collection.

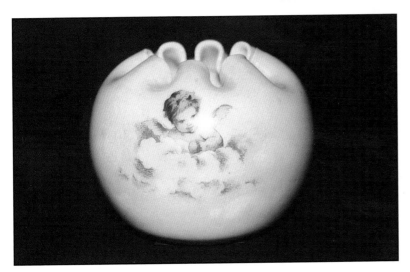

Fig. 372. This cherub is atypical in design, but still permanent. Collection of Ruth Sparks.

Fig. 373. Decals are generally factory-applied and fired for permanence. Photo courtesy of Larry and Kathy Murdie.

chapter two
THE EARLY TWENTIETH CENTURY
1910-1950s

There's no magic date that one can pinpoint to mark the end of the Victorian period and the beginning of a new style in glass. I chose to start the next section at 1910 because many of the Art Nouveau trends begun in the 1880s and 1890s continued well into the first decade of the twentieth century. The Art Nouveau period evolved slowly into Art Deco. Some rose bowl styles span both time periods, and in those cases I have put them in the section which I think best reflects their style.

Some of the following types of glass have been reproduced, particularly Carnival. Readers should be aware that, unlike Victorian glass which is more of a style, Carnival is a series of specific patterns and shapes. No one or two representative pieces can be used to illustrate differences between old and new as is done with Victorian art glass. Therefore, reproductions, which actually belong in Chapter 3, will be shown here so that side-by-side comparisons can be made.

Of course, I cannot show every single reproduction. Pay attention to the general clues given for discerning new from old, and study the examples so you can spot reproductions not shown or discussed in this book.

2.1. Carnival Glass

Carnival glass is defined as an iridescent pressed pattern glass, produced roughly between 1905 and 1930. In fact, some would say the important dates of Carnival production are 1907-1917, and that pieces produced later are not true Carnival. Regardless, Carnival was originally created to provide a more affordable alternative to Tiffany's iridescent favrile glass. Tiffany glass gets its iridescence from chemicals in the glass batch. In contrast, Carnival gets its iridescence from the much more economical use of a spray applied after the piece is made.

Although Carnival glass was made earlier, the stock market crash of 1929 did affect its history. As the country slipped further into the Great Depression, not even the common man could afford the cheap iridized wares so popular during the previous decade. Carnival glass ended up stockpiled, with no buyers. Barrels of it were given away to carnivals and movie theaters, where it was offered as a premium to customers, or as a prize. Its part in the carnivals of the day led to its name.

Carnival colors include marigold, blue, green, amethyst, white, and red, as well as some more obscure colors like smoke and teal. Some opalescent Carnival was also made. Most rose bowls are found in marigold, amethyst, green, blue, and white. Marigold is the most common color, and prices are generally lowest for this color. It's also one of the easiest colors to identify. Determining the color of red, blue, green, or amethyst pieces is harder because the iridescent highlights contain many hues. You must look inside, or at the base of the piece, to see the actual base color of the glass. Don't worry too much about spotting red, though, since only Fenton Coin Dot and Fenton Orange Tree rose bowls are known to exist in red Carnival.

Carnival was produced by many companies in the United States and abroad, but five U.S. companies are responsible for most of the Carnival production. They are Fenton, Imperial, Millersburg, Northwood, and Dugan. Of the five, Northwood and Fenton were the most prolific manufacturers of Carnival rose bowls.

Some Carnival rose bowls are crimped; some are not. Toes, collar bases, and even stems are prevalent among rose bowls produced in this type of glass. It might appear that rose bowls completely changed shape from the Victorian era, but they really did not. Most Victorian rose bowls are found in various types of art glass, and Carnival is pressed. Carnival rose bowl shapes are similar to those found in opalescent pattern glass, which was in its heyday about ten years before Carnival peaked in popularity. A few patterns are even found in both types of glass, including several patterns of rose bowls. Beaded Cable, and Daisy & Plume, are probably the most well-known of these crossovers.

That's not to say, however, that Carnival rose bowls are simply opalescent patterns with a different glass treatment. Although some Carnival patterns are similarly styled to opalescent ones, Carnival rose bowls, when considered as a group, do have a style all their own. A wide, squat shape is definitely more prevalent among rose bowls in Carnival than in opalescent glass. Some turn in only a tiny bit, just enough to be considered a rose bowl rather than just a bowl. Although some opalescent patterns didn't turn in all that much at the top, they tend to be taller, rather than short and squat like their Carnival cousins. Factors determining the value of Carnival rose bowls include the pattern and color, of course, but also the quality of the color and iridescence. Look for iridescence that is even and heavy, but not heavy enough that the piece looks brassy or white.

A combination of patterns can also sometimes be found in Carnival, but this doesn't appear to consistently impact price. It's more a matter of the buyer's taste. Beaded Cable, for

Fig. 374. Northwood's popular Beaded Cable pattern can be used to illustrate the most common colors in Carnival. This one is in marigold. Courtesy of Bruce Dooley and Evan Walker.

Fig. 375. Marigold with Stippled Rays interior. Note how the interior pattern changes the look of the piece. Courtesy of Bruce Dooley and Evan Walker.

Fig. 376. Beaded Cable, amethyst. Courtesy of Bruce Dooley and Evan Walker.

Fig. 377. Beaded Cable, blue. Courtesy of Bruce Dooley and Evan Walker.

example, is sometimes found with an interior Stippled Rays pattern, which gives the pattern a whole new look.

I will attempt to list as many Carnival patterns as I know exist in rose bowls. The names of the patterns seen on the market most often are in italics. Since I cannot illustrate every one, I suggest getting a good book on Carnival glass patterns and familiarizing yourself with the patterns listed below.

NORTHWOOD. *Beaded Cable* (marigold, amethyst, blue, green, peach opalescent, aqua opalescent, white). *Daisy & Plume* —both pedestal and three toed shapes—(marigold, amethyst, blue, green, aqua and blue opalescent, pastel). *Drapery* (marigold, amethyst, green, blue, aqua opalescent, white). *Fine Cut & Roses* (marigold, amethyst, green, blue, aqua opalescent, ice green).

NORTHWOOD-DUGAN. *Leaf & Beads* (marigold, amethyst, green, blue, aqua opalescent, white). Smooth Rays (marigold, amethyst, peach opalescent).

DUGAN. Fluted Scroll (amethyst). Four Flowers (believed to be Dugan, amethyst). Golden Grapes (marigold). *Grape Delight* (marigold, amethyst, blue, white). *Honeycomb* (marigold, peach opalescent). Ski Star (peach opalescent). *Small Rib* (stemmed: marigold, amethyst, green, amber).

FENTON. Beaded Stars (marigold). Coin Dot (marigold, red). *Garland* (marigold, amethyst, blue). Holly (marigold, green, blue). Horse's Heads (marigold, blue, Vaseline). Mirrored Lotus (marigold, blue, white). *Orange Tree* (marigold, amethyst, green, blue, white, red). *Persian Medallion* (marigold, amethyst, blue, green). Stag and Holly (marigold, green, blue). Two Flowers (marigold, green, blue). Vintage (marigold, blue).

NORTHWOOD OR FENTON. Inverted Coin Dot (marigold, green, pastel).

IMPERIAL. Diamond Ring (rare, marigold, amethyst, smoke). Fashion (rare, marigold, amethyst, green). Floral and Optic (peach opalescent, aqua). Frosted Block (marigold, clambroth). Garden Path variant (marigold). Grape (marigold, amethyst, green). Hattie (marigold, amber). Lustre Rose (marigold, amethyst, green, clambroth). Pillar and Flute (marigold, smoke). *Star & File* (marigold, amethyst, green, amber). Three-in-One (marigold). Waffle Block (marigold).

MILLERSBURG. Big Fish (rare, pastel). Deep Grape (stemmed, green). Fleur de Lis (rare, amethyst). *Hobnail* (marigold, amethyst, green). Hobnail Variant (marigold). Hobstar and Feather (marigold, green). Holly Sprig or Whirl (Vaseline). Nesting Swan (marigold). Peacock (amethyst). *Swirl Hobnail* (marigold, amethyst, blue).

Fig. 378. Beaded Cable, green. Note the Stippled Rays interior. Courtesy of Bruce Dooley and Evan Walker.

Fig. 379. Beaded Cable, ice blue. Courtesy of Ar-Jo Antiques and Horatio Antiques.

WESTMORELAND. Coin Dot variant (marigold, amethyst, teal). Concave Flute (marigold, blue, amethyst). *Louisa* (marigold, amethyst, green, blue, horehound).

OTHER. Aztec (McKee, rare, clambroth). Brocaded Acorns (Fostoria and related, pastel). Cane and Scroll (English, marigold, peach opalescent). Classic Arts (Czech, marigold). Cosmos and Cane (U.S. Glass, marigold, amethyst, amber). Daisy Square (unknown, marigold, amethyst, soft green). Fostoria #1231 (pastel). Hobstar and Cut Triangles (English, marigold, amethyst, green). (U.S. Glass, marigold). Kokomo (English, marigold, green, blue). Oval Star and Fan (Jenkins, marigold, amethyst). Palm Beach (U.S. Glass, marigold). Paneled Swirl (unknown, marigold). Pineapple (English, marigold). Rose Garden (Swedish, two sizes, small marigold, large, blue). Star & Hobs, (unknown, blue). Vining Leaf and Variant (English, marigold).

As with just about everything else, Carnival glass has been reproduced. The colors found in the 1960s and later Carnival glass are more brash, and not as deep. Newer Carnival also lacks the depth of iridescence found on older pieces. A piece of new blue Carnival, for example, looks blue from a distance. There is virtually no need to look at the base or the feet to see the true color of the glass underneath the iridescence.

Many of the newer pieces are also marked with a company trademark or logo. Aware that its older products had a market with collectors, Fenton began marking its new items with the company name in the early 1970s, or with a scripted "F" inside an oval. Imperial began marking its glassware with the letters "IG," one on top of the other, in the 1950s.

Of course, a marked piece is not necessarily always a new piece. Northwood marked many of its original Carnival pieces with a capital "N" inside a circle. The company no longer exists, and a collector's group now owns this trademark to prevent its improper use on new items.

 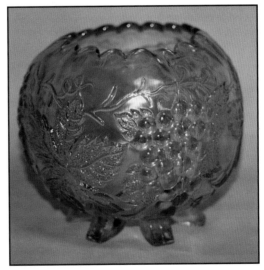

Fig. 380. Dugan's Grape Delight rose bowl in white. Courtesy of Grandma Patty's Antiques.

Fig. 381. LG Wright's "Grape" pattern is a reproduction of Dugan's Grape Delight. The Wright versions are not crimped. Courtesy of Leslie and Howard Diehl.

Fig. 383. Dugan's Grape Delight in
amethyst. Courtesy of Bruce Dooley
and Evan Walker.

Fig. 382. The Star & File pattern shows
off the typical shape of Imperial Carnival
rose bowls. Courtesy of Leslie and
Howard Diehl.

Fig. 384. Rare amber Imperial Grape rose
bowl. Courtesy of Ar-Jo Antiques and
Horatio Antiques.

Right: Fig. 385. Westmoreland's Louisa, in
teal. Collection of Stu Horn.

Northwood patterns are among those most frequently copied. Fenton produced many versions of Northwood's Drapery pattern, for example, in both Carnival and opalescent. Even without the company name on the piece, Fenton Drapery rose bowls are easy to spot, thanks to small changes made in the original design. Original Northwood Drapery rose bowls have a collar or wafer foot. Fenton's version, whether made in opalescent, Carnival, or some other type of glass, has toes.

In addition to Drapery, patterns known to have been reproduced in rose bowls include the following:

DUGAN'S GRAPE DELIGHT. The L.G. Wright Glass Co. purchased many old Dugan molds and produced their first Carnival in the 1960s. Their version of Grape Delight, which they simply call "Grape," is easy to spot because it is not crimped. Instead, it has a turned-in scalloped top. Although the crimping is the main key here, you will also notice that Wright versions lack the depth of color and iridescence of their older predecessors. Known Wright colors are amethyst, white, yellow, and green, with other colors possible. Dugan did not make this pattern in yellow or green.

Fig. 386. Westmoreland's Concave Flute, amethyst. Author's collection.

MILLERSBURG SWIRL HOBNAIL. Fenton made its own version of this pattern, too. In addition to being marked, the colors on the copies stand out much more than they do on originals, and there is less iridescence.

NORTHWOOD LEAF AND BEADS. Fenton has also cashed in on the popularity of this Northwood pattern, although their version is not limited to Carnival glass. Fenton rose bowls in this pattern are found in Rosalene (a pink and white glass) and Fenton's satin, in a variety of colors. Some Carnival examples are found now and then. They will generally bear the company signature, and although the iridescence on these is better than most, it is still not nearly as rich as the originals.

IMPERIAL. I don't list pattern names here because I am not sure how many Imperial rose bowls were made in the 1960s. But I do know that some were. Look for bright new gloss, colors that weren't originally made or that are uncommon in old Carnival, and the IG Imperial mark.

Fig. 387. Fenton's Orange Tree pattern, often referred to as "Fenton Flowers." Marigold. Courtesy of Leslie and Howard Diehl.

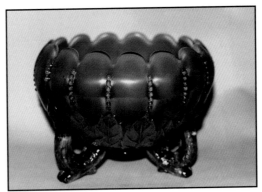

Fig. 388. Aqua Opalescent is one of the hardest to find and most desirable colors in Carnival glass. This one is in Northwood's Leaf and Beads pattern. Courtesy of Ar-Jo Antiques and Horatio Antiques.

Fig. 389. Bottom of Concave Flute.

Fig. 390. Westmoreland's Concave Flute in marigold.
Author's collection.

Fig. 391. Northwood's Drapery in ice blue.
Note the collar foot. Fenton reproductions
stand on three toes. Courtesy of Ar-Jo
Antiques and Horatio Antiques.
(See Fig. 548)

Fig. 392. Millersburg's Swirl Hobnail is one of the most desirable
patterns in Carnival rose bowls. Courtesy of Ar-Jo Antiques and
Horatio Antiques.

Fig. 393. This is the Fenton copy of Swirl Hobnail. They're pretty
close in shape, though the Fenton version is a little wider at the
top, compared to a more spherical original. Fenton copies are also
likely to bear the company logo. Collection of Stu Horn.

Fig. 395. Fenton Garland in marigold. Author's collection.

Fig. 394. Toed Daisy & Plume, amethyst. Courtesy of Leslie and Howard Diehl.

Fig. 396. Fenton Two Flowers. Courtesy of Theresa Brantley.

Fig. 397. Daisy & Plume in green, with Stippled Rays interior. Collection of Martha Ross.

Fig. 398. White Northwood Fine Cut &
Roses. Collection of Martha Ross.

Right: Fig. 400. Marigold Northwood Fine
Cut & Roses. Collection of Martha Ross.

Fig. 399. Dugan's Wreath of Roses. Courtesy of Theresa Brantley.

2.2. Depression Glass

When most people hear the term "Depression glass," they correctly think of mass-produced colored glassware made in America during the 1930s. But it goes back a bit farther than that. Colored glass tableware had actually become the rage in the 1920s, but only the more affluent could afford it. During this decade, some companies began making certain items by machine, sparking debate over whether such items could be considered a legitimate part of the glass-making art.

After the stock market crashed, the thirst for colored glass continued, and, with timing nothing short of perfect, glass makers expanded their lines of inexpensive, mass-produced colored tableware. Suddenly, the average person could own colored glass, which was given away as premiums or sold for nickels and dimes. The state of the economy had effectively addressed concerns over whether machine-made glass had a future. Back then, people collected their sets one piece at a time, just as collectors do today.

Most people probably don't think of rose bowls when they think of Depression glass. Rose bowls were still around when the stock market crashed, though they weren't as popular as they had been in the Victorian era. Although some Depression-era patterns included rose bowls, the vast majority did not.

The shape of most Depression-era rose bowls was derived from the precedents set by Carnival glass. By the mid-1920s, the rose bowl had grown toes, and opened itself up like the flowers its Victorian predecessors held. In many instances, Depression-era rose bowls became heart-shaped, starting from a narrow bottom and widening until just below the rim. The very top edges turn-in slightly, narrowing the width of the rim. Most have six to eight points, which jut-up above the run about 1/4 inch, coming back down again rather sharply, before lazily flowing into the next point. This rather smooth rim bears only a hint of the crimped and scalloped tops so commonly associated with Victorian rose bowls. Lancaster's Jubilee (see fig. 416) and the L.E. Smith Glass Company's Mt. Pleasant rose bowls are good examples of this shape.

Even if not exactly this shape, most Depression-era rose bowls are some variant of it. Westmoreland's English Hobnail, for example, is not toed but is still heart-shaped. Like English Hobnail, many other Depression-era rose bowls have a collar foot and somewhat squat shape.

Of course, not all Depression-era rose bowls have this open shape. Some, such as the one in Fostoria's Baroque line, can be found on a collar foot, rather than toes. The Baroque rose bowl is a rather unusual Depression glass rose bowl because it's actually very round, with a scalloped top.

Fig. 401. Cambridge Caprice rose bowls come in two sizes and several colors including blue, pink, and crystal. This one is courtesy of John Corl and the Elegant Glass Collectors Club.

Fig. 402. Jasmine (yellow opalescent) Duncan & Miller Canterbury. Courtesy of Precious & Few.

Fig. 403. Duncan & Miller Canterbury, Cape Cod (blue opalescent). Opalescent colors date to 1940s. Author's collection.

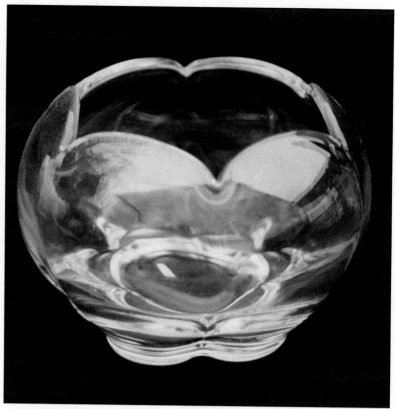

Fig. 404. Since this example is in crystal, there is no way to know if it is a Duncan & Miller or Tiffin piece. Author's collection.

Fig. 405. Duncan & Miller originally called this shape a "footed violet vase." But with crimps, collectors will accept it as a stemmed rose bowl. A non-crimped version was also made. I've seen these in crystal, ruby, and Cape Cod Blue, though other Duncan colors are apt to be seen. Collection of Frank B. Strovel, Jr.

Fig. 406. Imperial Omero is one of the few Depression patterns found with real crimps. Blanks in this pattern are also found, and usually only in pink. Author's collection.

In addition to Westmoreland and L.E. Smith, already named, the primary producers of Depression-era rose bowls were Fenton, Fostoria, Imperial, Lancaster, and Heisey, with a few also made by Cambridge, Duncan & Miller, and Standard.

Of all the companies, Fenton and Imperial probably made the biggest variety of rose bowls. Fenton made a few round ones called "rose bowls," but the company called many of its rose bowl-shaped pieces from this era "cupped bowls." These generally stand on a collar foot or on three toes, and are squat or heart-shaped.

Imperial made a variety of different rose bowls, some called "rose bowls," others called "lily bowls." Beaded Block, Monticello, Amelia, Lindburgh, and the Scroll Fluted patterns all have a piece in the pattern called a "lily bowl." These are shaped much like Fenton's "cupped bowls." The Omero pattern has a rose bowl in a similar shape to Beaded Block and the other "lily bowls," but interestingly, it's called a "rose bowl."

Many companies would use the same blank for more than one line, changing only the decoration. Duncan & Miller's First Love pattern, which includes a rose bowl, is merely one particular etching on that same pattern blank. Imperial used its Molly blanks for a variety of etchings. Some companies would even make the glass and have another company decorate it. As a result, collectors can occasionally find undecorated Depression glass rose bowl blanks.

Interestingly, it seems few Depression-era rose bowls were made in the mass-produced colored patterns. Most of the relative few that exist were at least partially handmade, often by companies known for their "elegant" lines.

Naturally, all rose bowls of the Depression era are found in the usual colors, including pink, yellow, blue, and green. Many can also be found in crystal, black, ruby, and cobalt. Each company had its own name for each of its colors, so you may see these colors called by different names.

Fig. 407. I don't have the pattern name identified here, but this is a McKee shape. Courtesy of Leslie and Howard Diehl.

Fig. 408. Heisey made a few rose bowls in its time, too. This one is in the Tourjours pattern, shown courtesy of Robert Bartholomew.

Fig. 409. Fostoria began production of its American pattern during the Depression, but the pattern continued to be made right up to the factory's closing in the 1980s. Collection of Martha Ross.

Fig. 410. Blanks in this shape are identified in old Imperial catalogs as "Molly." They're found in green, pink, yellow, and black amethyst. This shape is also found etched and given a variety of pattern names including Corona, Monticello, and Viking. Author's collection.

Fig. 411. Imperial Molly blank with the Viking etch. Photo courtesy of Karen Comer.

Fig. 412. It isn't exactly Molly, but there's no doubt that this is Imperial.

Fig. 413. Close-up of Fostoria's Baroque, in crystal.

Fig. 414. Imperial Molly blank in black amethyst with floral decoration. The name of the design is unknown. Author's collection.

Fig. 415. Fostoria's Baroque rose bowls are nicely rounded and spherical. They come in crystal, yellow (topaz), and azure blue. Author's collection.

As with rose bowls from other time periods, some confusion exists over which Depression pieces are rose bowls, and which are not. In fact, rose bowls of the Depression era are the most difficult to identify since manufacturers during this time period were particularly inconsistent with their nomenclature. Size has no bearing on the names.

Imperial's "lily bowls" range in size from 5 to 8 inches in diameter. Imperial's Omero "rose bowl" is also about 5 inches. McKee gives the name "rose bowl" to its 8-inch Beacon Innovative Cut rose bowl. This kind of inconsistency is one of the reasons collectors have trouble defining the term "rose bowl."

Colored glass began to fall out of favor in the 1940s. Crystal was back. A few companies, such as Heisey, continued to have success with their colored wares, but the days of mass-produced colored tableware came to an end with the end of the 1940s.

Collectors should be aware, however, that just because a pattern was made in "Depression glass" does not mean that all pieces found in that pattern were made between the early 1920s and late 1940s. Many patterns introduced during the Depression era continued to be made until much later. For example, Fostoria's Colony pattern, which includes a rose bowl, was made into the 1970s; and American, another pattern which includes rose bowls, was made right up until the company's closing in the 1980s.

Confusion also exists over patterns made by one company during the Depression and then produced by another company somewhat later. Duncan & Miller's Canterbury pattern is one such example. The company made this pattern, including rose bowls, from 1937 to 1955. The U.S. Glass Company's factory in Tiffin, Ohio, acquired the Canterbury molds in 1955, and continued to produce the pattern. Clues as to who made what are found in the colors. Duncan colors included crystal, ruby, pale blue, chartreuse (transparent greenish-yellow), Cape Cod (blue opalescent), Cranberry pink (pink opalescent), and Jasmine (yellow opalescent), with the opalescent colors being added in the 1940s. Tiffin's colors include crystal, Twilight (transparent lavender), Killarney (dark green), Wistaria (rosy red to pink), and Dawn (alexandrite). If it's crystal, there's no way to tell, however.

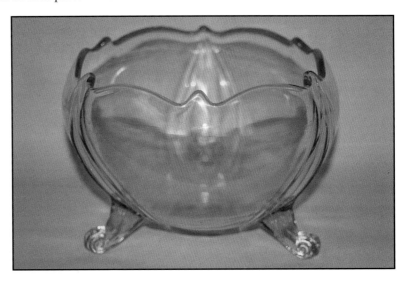

Fig. 416. Lancaster blank for etched Jubilee pattern. Also found in pink and with other etchings. Author's collection.

Canterbury is one of the few Depression-era patterns made in any kind of opalescent color. A few opalescent rose bowls were made by Imperial, in its Beaded Block pattern, which dates to the late 1920s and early 1930s. It was called a lily bowl, though. Laced Edge is another Depression-era Imperial opalescent pattern. When the laced edges are turned inward rather than outward, you could consider this a rose bowl, though it is not the most attractive of styles.

The main patterns found in Depression rose bowls are as follows. Note that with etched patterns, other etchings may also be found.

Cambridge: Mt. Vernon, Caprice. **Duncan & Miller:** Canterbury, First Love. **Fostoria:** American, Baroque, Colony. **Heisey:** Rose, Victorian. **Hocking:** Miss America. **Imperial:** Amelia, Beaded Block, Diamond Block, Katy, Laurel, Lindburgh, Monticello, Pillar Fluted and Scroll Fluted. **Lancaster:** Jubilee, Jubilee blank, Carolyn, Landrum. **L.E. Smith:** Mt. Pleasant. **McKee:** Beacon Innovative Cut. **Paden City:** Lela Bird. **Standard:** 5-inch footed rose bowl (no pattern name). **Westmoreland:** English Hobnail.

2.3. American Art Glass

Although the Great Depression had a strong enough influence on the glass industry to create a whole new phenomenon in glass, the stacks of a few art glass departments continued to burn.

Imperial created a line of art glass beginning in the 1920s called "Free Hand," and this line included a rose bowl that stands on a short pedestal base and is not crimped. The line was created to find new outlets, since the market for its machine-made wares was declining. Imperial Free Hand was not very successful, but it remained in the line until 1931, when the company fell into bankruptcy and reorganized.

The same shape is found in Durand art glass, made by the Vineland Flint Glassworks in Vineland, New Jersey. Vineland Flint art glass had a short life, due to the accidental death of Victor Durand, Jr., in a car accident in 1931. The company had only begun to produce art glass seven years earlier, in 1924.

Durand rose bowls come in a variety of colors and patterns, most of which are iridescent. Some cut and engraved colored glass rose bowls were also produced.

Vineland Flint merged with the Kimble Glass Company in 1931, and Kimble produced a non-crimped egg-shaped rose bowl in its Cluthra glass until about 1933. Because of the Depression, however, art glass did not sell, and it was finally discontinued.

FENTON. During this time of economic turmoil, Fenton had a line of quality art glass. The company started out with Carnival shortly after its founding, but was making art glass by 1925, alongside Imperial and Durand. Stretch glass rose bowls appeared in 1927, though these are quite hard to find. You're more likely to see the larger, more squat "cupped bowls," which meet the general definition of a rose bowl than you are the smaller designs, which the company did call rose bowls.

The custard Persian Medallion rose bowl actually appeared somewhat earlier, in 1915. Interestingly, it is found with a square opening, while the somewhat earlier Carnival version has a round opening, according to old catalogs. Persian Medallion rose bowls with square openings are also found in Persian Blue, c. 1915. The Silvertone pattern, etched and molded into colored transparent glass, is found in a three-toed Depression rose bowl shape, and dates to 1936-1937. (And they called it a cupped bowl!) This shape appears in other patterns, too, around the same time.

Fig. 417. One of a number of styles of Durand rose bowls. Courtesy of Arlene Rabin Antiques.

Fig. 418. The Imperial Free Hand rose bowl shares the Durand shape. Courtesy of Dottie Freeman and Allan Teal.

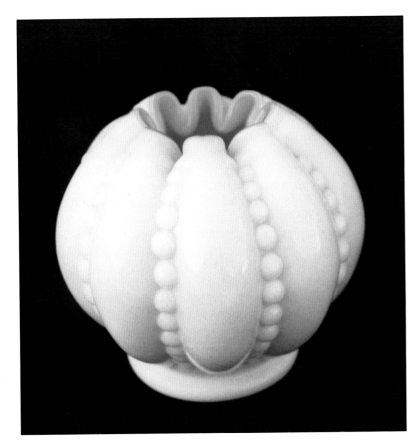

Fig. 419. Kimble Cluthra rose bowl in blue. Also found in gold and green, among other colors. Collection of Frank B. Strovel, Jr.

Fig. 420. Fenton's Beaded Melon rose bowls come in gold and two shades of green, all with a white interior, and in white with a yellow interior. Author's collection.

In terms of rose bowl production, Fenton came into its own in the late 1930s and early 1940s with hobnail, opalescent glass, and overlay. Some of those familiar to collectors include Beaded Melon in ivy green, lighter green, gold, and white, with a yellow interior, c. 1949-1951; opalescent hobnail in white, blue, green, and cranberry, starting in 1949; Ivory and Silver Crest, starting in the 1940s; and spiral opalescent in cranberry, white, and possibly green, starting in 1939.

Some etched patterns also were made into rose bowls, including Pointsettia and Twin Ivy. These are the most common patterns found in rose bowls. Other patterns can be found in the many references that exist on this company.

Just as shape has long been a clue to identifying rose bowls by makers such as Thomas Webb and Mt. Washington, it can be used to identify Fenton rose bowls. Whether you include Fenton rose bowls in your collection or not, familiarity with them, and the ability to properly identify them, is essential.

Although Fenton's rose bowl shape varies, as do the rose bowls of every company, the majority are spherical and stand on a collar or wafer foot. They typically have eight crimps, and when viewed from above, the crimps resemble an eight-point star. I've nicknamed this "the Fenton star," and have used it to show beginners one way of identifying Fenton rose bowls.

So far, every rose bowl I have found in this shape has proven to be Fenton, with the exception of rose bowls made by Fenton for L.G. Wright (these are discussed in the next chapter). You should be aware that not every Fenton rose bowl is found in this shape. The company gets credit from collectors for producing far more rose bowls than they actually did, despite the fact that Fenton glass is widely studied and recognized.

A few Fenton rose bowls are not crimped at all, but have scalloped or smooth rims. These include some newer colored-glass rose bowls made to resemble early pattern glass designs. They often come with a votive candle. Fenton also made a squat miniature, as well

Fig. 421. The "Fenton star."

as some spherical 3-1/2-inch examples, with only six crimps. And, the company's popular lily-of-the-valley design has eight scallops and a squat, rather than spherical, shape. Most of these are late models, produced after 1960, and a sampling is shown in Chapter 3.

Regardless of shape variation, all but two Fenton rose bowls have some kind of foot, whether a collar or wafer foot or toes. The two exceptions are Robert Barber's Cascade Vase, which is shaped like a rose bowl even though it was not originally called one, and the company's Beatty Honeycomb rose bowl, which is tall and cylindrical, with a crimped top. The Barber vase, which dates to 1976, is the largest one shown on this book's cover. The Beatty Honeycomb rose bowl is illustrated in Section 3, since it was made in 1960.

Although it's difficult to accurately date a single piece of Fenton hobnail, some shape variations do exist to help the collector discern a newer Fenton hobnail rose bowl from the older ones, which were made starting in the 1940s. The older Fenton opalescent hobnail rose bowls tend to be rounder than their contemporary counterparts, which are more egg shaped by comparison. More modern colors, such as a light pink, also provide clues when a piece is not particularly old.

I've noticed that those who specialize in Victorian art glass have a tendency to think that anything they can't identify must be Fenton. The company made a lot of rose bowls, but not every anomaly is Fenton. Look for identifying traits such as the Fenton star, collar foot, and even the Fenton mark. If these are absent, consider all possibilities before concluding that the rose bowl in question is a Fenton.

Fig. 422. Fenton made a name for itself in the 1940s with hobnail opalescent glass. Vintage Fenton opalescent hobnail rose bowls come in two sizes and are found in white, blue, green, Vaseline, and cranberry. The small ones measure almost 3" and the larger ones almost 5". The small ones were in the catalog for only a short time in 1950. Author's collection.

2.4. European Art Glass

A completely different set of world events, not directly related to the economic scene in the United States, affected glass makers in other parts of the globe. Instead of a stock market crash, which greatly impacted the glass making industry in America, these foreign glass houses had World Wars and their own politics to contend with. Nevertheless, much more art glass was produced abroad than in America during this period, though the number of rose bowls wasn't exceedingly great.

All of the rose bowls produced by these overseas firms, when considered in total, is probably about equal to the entire rose bowl output of Fenton!

Rossler. In Bohemia, World War I made enamel used for glass decorating a hard-to-come-by commodity. Theodor Rossler used second-rate pre-war enamel cakes to create a new decorating technique which involved puddles of colored enamel. The discovery was quite by accident, since he had hoped the enamel would work as it had before the war, when it was still fresh.

Fig. 423. Rossler rose bowls have enameled figures against a gilded background. This design is on one of the 5" examples. Collection of Martha Ross.

Rossler decorated rose bowls and other shapes in glass with enameled people against a background scene outlined in gold, but otherwise colorless, thereby making the figures really stand out. Rossler was a decorator, not a glass maker, who used blanks that I believe to be of German origin. These blanks can be found in both glass and ceramic, and on occasion, the ceramic ones are signed "Germany." Although the blanks are sometimes found in 2-inch sizes, Rossler is known to have decorated only the 3-inch and 5-inch sizes in crystal, cranberry, amethyst, and a pea green, with green and cranberry being the most common. All have polished bottoms and six crimps, often highlighted in gold. The bodies of the bowls are often found with fine ribbing.

Fig. 424. Shot of the whole bowl (left) shown in fig. 423.

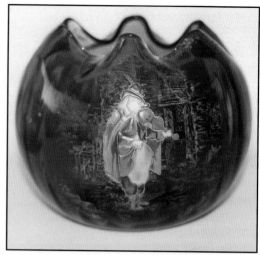

Fig. 425. You don't find Rossler rose bowls in amethyst too often. 5" tall. Collection of Martha Ross.

Fig. 426. Cranberry example in the 3" size. Author's collection.

Fig. 427. Another example in the large green. Collection of Stu Horn.

Fig. 428. The style of enameling on this amethyst mini is typical of Moser, c. 1910-1930. Rossler did this style of enameling, but thus far only figures are known, and no rose bowls in this size are known, either. 2" tall. Author's collection.

Fig. 429. A crystal example with the same design as Fig. 428. 2" tall. Collection of Stu Horn.

Fig. 430. Neither Rossler nor Moser made these blanks, which are identical in size and shape to blanks I've seen marked "Germany." Who did the decoration on this one is also a mystery. In any event, a sailboat is an unusual decoration for a rose bowl. 2" high. Author's collection.

They also usually have an odd mark that looks something like a scripted "E." I haven't been able to verify that this is, indeed, a Rossler signature.

Orrefors. This Swedish company, established in 1898, began by producing glass windows and ink bottles before venturing into high-quality crystal in 1913. Orrefors made seven different sizes of rose bowls, starting with a tiny 2-inch version.

Orrefors signs all its work, except for seconds, and the rose bowls have polished bottoms. The signatures are found on the outside edges of the bottoms and are usually small. They typically begin with the letters "Of" which are sometimes difficult to read. I thought the scripted "Of" was a fancy "A" the first time I saw it. Following those letters will be shape numbers and initials, which refer to the person who made the form and designed the decoration. The rose bowl form most often found was designed by Vicke Lindstrand. Edward Hald designed the etched butterflies and birds found on these examples.

French cameo. This trend in Art Nouveau glass began in about 1890, and lasted to nearly the mid-twentieth century, which is why it is placed in this section of the book. In addition, the majority of French cameo rose bowls date to 1910 and later.

The producers of French cameo never intended for their creations to compete with English cameo. Instead, their cameo was intended to create an entirely new subtle art form, utilizing color and shape.

Aside from Galle, who did not make rose bowls, probably the most famous of the French cameo glass makers are the Daum brothers, Auguste and Antonin, who were originally from Lorraine. Their best work dates to about 1890. Rose bowls by these brothers are few and far between, though I did once see a very tiny, 1-inch miniature, mentioned in the section on miniatures in the last chapter.

The two types of French cameo rose bowls most often encountered are Legras and Mont Joye.

August Legras' company, which went by the name of Legras et Cie, was located in St. Denis, France, and the firm's designs often incorporated both enamel and cameo to create true-to-life scenes. The company closed down in 1914 because of World War I, and reopened in 1919. Post-war production included pseudo-cameo in florals, and landscapes with a mottled surface created by an acid treatment. Geometric Art Deco designs showed up on rose bowls in the 1920s and 1930s.

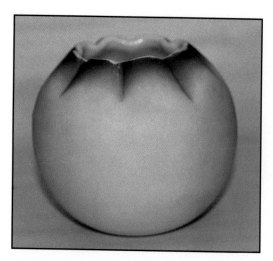

Fig. 431. This gritty satin rose bowl has a ground pontil and is marked "Czecho Slovak." Author's collection.

Fig. 434. This miniature, marked "Made in Czecho Slovakia" stands only 1-7/8" high. This design is found in other shapes. Author's collection.

Fig. 435. On the other hand, this one stands a good 6" tall. It's Loetz. Collection of Ruth Sparks.

Mont Joye is not actually a company, but just one of a number of signatures used by another company. Just which company is not clear, since references tend to contradict each other. Some sources connect the mark with Cristallerie de Pantin. Others connect the mark with Legras et Cie. Either way, it's definitely French. I was unable to locate dates of production for the mark. Since many other makers of French cameo rose bowls, including several lesser-known ones, seem to be from this period, I believe this is the most fitting section for Mont Joye examples.

Of course, the European rose bowls produced during this time frame are not necessarily limited to the above. However, I believe we've covered the most important and prolific makers of rose bowls.

Figs. 432 and 433. These miniature blanks are found in unfrosted cranberry and light green, among other colors. Author's collection.

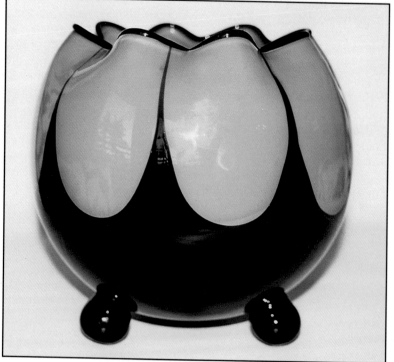

Fig. 436. Large, heavy crystal Orrefors.
The "F" in the signature indicates it
was designed by Edvin Orhstrom.
Author's collection.

Fig. 437. Trio of Orrefors miniatures. The one in the back stands
3" tall. The bird was designed by Edward Hald in 1941. The form
was designed by Vicke Lindstrand. The butterfly design was also
by Hald. 2" high. These were made in seven sizes. The undecorated one is a second. Author's collection.

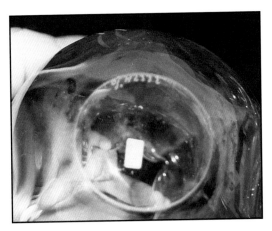

Fig. 438. Signature on the bird Orrefors
rose bowl.

Fig. 439. Signature on the butterfly Orrefors bowl.

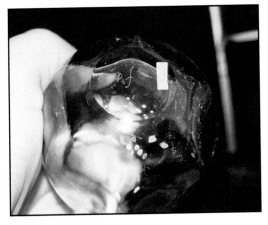

Fig. 440. Forged signature on the
Orrefors second.

Fig. 441. Legras rose bowl.

Fig. 442. Large Legras bowl. Collection of Ruth Sparks.

Fig. 443. This French miniature is not signed, but is nicely done. Collection of Ruth Sparks.

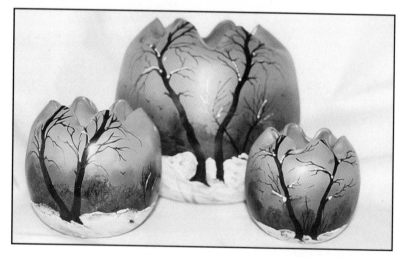

Fig. 444. Shown are three of at least five sizes found in this Legras design. Collection of Ruth Sparks.

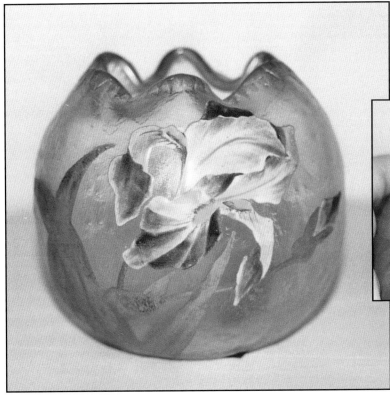

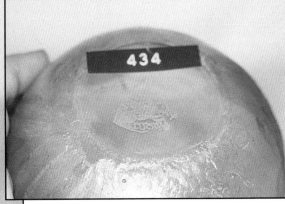

Fig. 445. Mont Joye mark.

Fig. 446. Mont Joye rose bowl with iris.
Collection of Ruth Sparks.

Fig. 447. The St. Denis mark. This mark is
not identified as being used by a particular
company. It is not uncommon for glass to
be named for the area in which it was
made. Since Legras was located in St.
Denis, a northern suburb of Paris, Legras
is the probable maker.

Fig. 448. Giant French cameo-style
bowl marked St. Denis. Collection of
Ruth Sparks.

Fig. 449. The geometric pattern on this cut-to-clear rose bowl indicates it is from the Deco period. Collection of Frank B. Strovel, Jr.

Fig. 450. "Peynaun" is derived from the name of the company, Peynaud, combined with Nancy—an area in France. Collection of Martha Ross.

Above & Lower Right: Figs. 451-452. The English firm, Bagerly, made these in two sizes and several colors. Gold: Author's collection. Blue: Collection of Stu Horn.

Above: Fig. 453. I'm honestly not sure how old these paperweight-style rose bowls are. Author's and Stu Horn's collections.

2.5. Ceramic Rose Bowls

Although most rose bowls are made of glass, a small number can be found in ceramics, including china, porcelain, and even pottery. China, porcelain, and pottery items are beyond the intended scope of this book, and for that reason I will attempt to provide only some basic information about these rose bowls. I have not been able to date most of them, though I imagine more could be done by studying these materials in more depth—much the same way that I have studied glass. Since that was not practical for this volume, I decided to include these materials in the middle section of the book. I chose to do so primarily because one of my favorite china rose bowls is dated 1923, which puts it solidly in this section. This item is a gold art deco piece marked in green with a crown, the letters "TK," and then the word "Czechoslovakia." It is signed "H Ludeman '23 to Mother." Even if it weren't signed, we would know it was made sometime after 1918, which is when the Bohemian kingdom fell and Czechoslovakia became a country.

Another reason for putting china and porcelain rose bowls in this chapter is because choosing the middle of the road is usually a more safe approach! As new information evolves, it is somewhat easier to make the adjustment to an earlier or later period. Some china rose bowls are pictured in the other two chapters if they are known to date to those specific time periods. You should be aware that not all of the china, porcelain, and pottery rose bowls pictured in this chapter definitely were made in the first half of the twentieth century. I suggest further in-depth study of china, porcelain, and pottery if you wish to accurately date them.

The first time I ever saw a rose bowl produced in china was when I purchased one with a lighthouse on it. Since I didn't have a clue where to start in identifying this piece, I turned to *AntiqueWeek's* "World of Ceramics" columnists, Susan and Jim Harran. They were able to identify my item as a piece of pre-Nippon Japanese porcelain. This put its birth date somewhere in the 1880s. (This piece is illustrated in Chapter 1). Fine Japanese ceramics imported from 1891-1921 were marked "Nippon," in accordance with U.S. import laws. The bowl, the Harrans believe, was quite possibly exported by the Morimura Brothers, who

Fig. 454. This example, marked with a crown, the letters "R" and "C," and the word "Bavaria," was made by Philip Rosenthal & Co. The mark was used from 1901-1956.

Fig. 455. Miniature advertising piece for the National Cash Register Co. It's identical in size and shape to the glass rose bowls shown in figs. 428-430, 432, 433. Author's collection.

Fig. 456. This example, which has a creamy iridescent interior, was made between 1918 and 1930 by Graeflick Thunsche Porzellanfabrick, in Bohemia. It is signed "H. Ludeman '23 to Mother." 4-1/2" high. Author's collection.

had offices in New York, and who provided this country with some of Japan's finest porcelains. Decorations such as those on my piece frequently combined western scenes and Japanese florals. *The Collector's Encyclopedia of Nippon Porcelain* series, by Joan F. Van Patten, pictures several rose bowls made during the first half of the twentieth century and during the 1950s.

I have since found a number of china and porcelain rose bowls, and they are among the most interesting and intriguing of bowls. According to "World of Ceramics," at that time only two china/porcelain rose bowls were documented as being made in Europe. A crimped bowl resembling a rose bowl is shown in *Collector's Encyclopedia of Pickard China*, by Alan B. Reed. This piece, made from 1903-1905, is a Limoges blank decorated by the Pickard studio, and described in the book as a "cache or ferner." Royal Bayreuth also produced a 4-inch rose bowl picturing a man fishing in a wooded setting. But these are by no means the only ones. The existing reference books may not cover them, but they do exist. A number of china and porcelain rose bowls have come—or are coming from, as the case may be—Austria, Czechoslovakia, and Germany.

The German rose bowls are miniatures, with six crimps, and they stand 2 inches high. For the most part, they are advertising pieces. Most are unmarked, but I have seen some marked "Germany."

What's intriguing is the fact that these miniature advertising examples in porcelain are identical in size and shape to a number of miniature rose bowls found in glass. These are found in a variety of colors, including amethyst, cranberry, light green, and crystal. Some are decorated. Others are not.

This observation can be taken a step further. The miniatures, whether glass or china, all match the shape of Rossler rose bowls found in two larger sizes (see section 2.4). Rossler, a Bohemian decorator, is known for enameled people shown against gold-outlined backgrounds. To my knowledge, Rossler did not make glass. It appears that he purchased blanks from the same company that produced the ceramic blanks. Or, the blanks he used may have been copied from the ceramic ones.

Before I go further, I should note that it's possible that the glass and ceramic blanks did not originate in the same place. I have on occasion, for example, encountered ceramic copies of Fenton and Northwood Carnival rose bowls. Frank M. Fenton has, himself, confirmed that Fenton never made porcelain or ceramic pieces, nor did the company license anyone else to make these items. But, at the moment, the German connection for the little six-crimped Bohemian rose bowls is perhaps the best clue to their origin.

Another group of china rose bowls can be found marked "Austria." The mark includes a wreath and the initials "O & EG," and the word "Royal." Thanks to assistance provided by some china and porcelain collectors and a Kovel book on marks, I have determined the mark is for Oscar and Edgar Gutherz, Royal Austria, 1899-1918. I have seen these rose bowls in a number of patterns. All measure 3 inches high and are about 3-3/4 inches across. All bear the same mark, plus a little bit of gold highlighting the rim.

I have also discovered a few china rose bowls by more well-known names in ceramics such as Belleek, Staffordshire, and Lefton.

Most of these china and porcelain rose bowls have very delicate soft crimps, kind of like those produced by Mt. Washington or Thomas Webb. It's unusual to find one with deep crimping, although they do exist. Most of the examples I have seen with deep crimps are Oriental in origin, based on the markings done with Oriental symbols.

I have also, on occasion, found some pottery rose bowls. Even fewer numbers of these exist, at least if you are looking for a spherical crimped example. Haeger made them, and so did Gonder. Roseville made something that most collectors seem to call a rose bowl, but it doesn't meet the definition created by glass collectors. A couple of examples are depicted here, but these items won't be treated in depth because, again, that is beyond the glass-oriented focus of this book. Nevertheless, it is important that collectors and dealers be aware that pottery examples do exist.

Fig. 457. The mark here is EIAPG, for Erste Porzellan-Industrie AG, and dates to between 1918 and 1945. Note the similarities in shape between this piece and the one shown in fig. 257. This company merged with several others in 1918, so perhaps the maker of the other bowl was part of that merger. Author's collection.

Fig. 458. This is a lovely Oriental bowl—unfortunately I am not able to accurately date it. Deep crimping is unusual in ceramic rose bowls. Author's collection.

Fig. 459. I may not be able to date the rose bowl, but I was able to determine that the bottom reads "Spring Light Manufacturer," thanks to the help of a colleague, Fei-Min Fann, who speaks and reads Chinese!

Fig. 460. Another Oriental example. Collection of Martha Ross.

Above & Left: Figs. 461-462. This piece is marked "Germany." Collection of David Billings.

Fig. 463. The people on this piece are similar to the ones in fig. 460. This example is not marked. Author's collection.

Fig. 464. Another unmarked example. About 3" high. Collection of Martha Ross.

Fig. 465. This piece is marked, but the mark remains unidentified. About 2" high. Collection of Martha Ross.

Fig. 466. The mark on the bowl in fig. 465.

Fig. 467. Another without a mark. This one is tiny—barely 2" tall—and cute in a flowerform. Collection of Martha Ross.

Fig. 468. Another complete mystery. About 5" high. Collection of Martha Ross.

Fig. 469. There are no marks on this piece, which looks like a sea urchin. Author's collection.

Fig. 470. This miniature, which stands about 2" tall, is also not marked. Collection of Martha Ross.

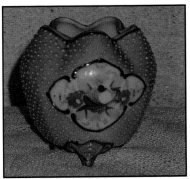

Fig. 471. This example is also not marked, but is probably by the same maker. Photo courtesy of Larry and Kathy Murdie.

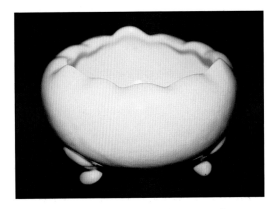

Fig. 472. Pottery rose bowl. Age and origin are unknown.

chapter three
LATE MODELS
SINCE 1960

It's no secret that rose bowls have been widely reproduced. But rose bowls that have actually been copied from earlier versions make up only a small fraction of the rose bowls produced in the last forty years. With that in mind, I have decided to call this section "Late Models" so I can cover originals that have been produced since 1960, as well as reproductions made in that same time frame. Many of these late model originals are quite beautiful and eminently collectible.

3.1. L.G. Wright

This company, founded in 1937 in New Martinsville, West Virginia, is still in business, so it stands to reason that a number of their rose bowls were made prior to 1960. Many of Wright's lines were long-running, which makes the dating of individual items difficult. However, I've placed discussion of the company in this later-models chapter since this includes the largest segment of their history. However, some Wright rose bowls are pictured in the previous section.

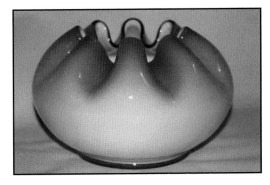

Fig. 473. This squat Wright shape is as distinctive as a signature. The cased pink/white glass is also Wright's peachblow. Author's collection.

Wright does not make its own glass, but instead contracts with other glass companies to make its glass with Wright molds. It is true that Fenton made much of the glass sold by Wright, and probably still does. But it's not necessary to identify the actual maker of a piece of Wright glass. Simply identifying it as Wright is enough, since that is what it truly is.

Two distinctive shapes mark Wright rose bowls as clearly as any signature—more clearly, in fact, since signatures can be forged (see section 3.8). One shape is squat, with a collar foot and eight crimps, measuring roughly 4-1/2 inches tall by 7-1/2 inches wide. The second shape is similar, but is spherical, not squat, and has six crimps instead of eight.

Wright rose bowls are most often misidentified as being Fenton. But Wright and Fenton rose bowls are not impossible to tell apart. In fact, all it takes to tell them apart is a little practice. Most Fenton rose bowls have eight crimps, where Wright rose bowls have six. However, a few of the Fenton styles made in recent years also have six crimps. So, it also helps to pay attention to crimp style as well as to crimp numbers in order to tell these apart. Wright crimps tend to be larger, higher, and wider than Fenton crimps.

It's important to note that some spherical Wright rose bowls are found with eight crimps. A few exhibit the Fenton star when viewed from above, and these are obviously made by Fenton for Wright. You can tell they were made for Wright, and were not part

Fig. 474. Wright's six-crimped shape comes in a variety of glass treatments. This tortoiseshell pattern is found in both glossy and matte finishes. Collection of Frank B. Strovel, Jr.

Left: Fig. 475. This is the second distinctive Wright shape. Note the collar foot and six crimps. Author's collection.

Fig. 476. Wright peachblow rose bowl with eight crimps and Moss Rose decoration. Collection of Stu Horn.

Fig. 477. This eight-crimped rose bowl has the Fenton star. But it is definitely a piece from the Wright line, in their "Honeycomb" pattern. Collection of Stu Horn.

Fig. 478. Wright Daisy and Fern. We know this is a Wright piece because of the matte finish. Also see fig. 241. Photo courtesy of Larry and Kathy Murdie.

Fig. 479. Wright's Thumbprint pattern is found in both squat and spherical eight-crimped shapes. Author's collection.

Fig. 480. Wright's Maize pattern rose bowls exhibit the Wright squat shape. Plus, they're all one color outside, generally cased, and crimped—all characteristics which you won't find on original Libbey Maize. Collection of Stu Horn.

Fig. 481. Can you pick out which of the three bowls is Fenton? It's the one on the right, recognizable as Fenton because the dots are staggered and do not go all the way up to the crimps. The one on the right is Wright's Eye Dot, and the center item is their Honeycomb. Photo courtesy of Stu Horn.

Fig. 482. Wright Thumbprint in green. This one was purchased in February 1998 at an auction of the Wright estate. Wright company owner Phyllis Stephan Buettner said it had been in the company or home attic for the previous 25 years. Author's collection.

Fig. 483. Wright currently offers blown slag and iridescent spatter rose bowls with eight crimps and a rough pontils. They retail for around $28 a piece. Author's collection.

Fig. 484. Wright copied Northwood's Opal Open, but changed the stem. Northwood's stem is open, for a pierced effect. Wright's stems are closed. Collection of Frank. B. Strovel, Jr.

of the regular Fenton line, by the patterns, which include Honeycomb and peachblow (cased white/pink, often with Wright's Moss Rose decoration). Some other Wright patterns are also found with eight crimps, but these do not exhibit the Fenton star. Who actually made them is unknown and probably irrelevant.

Wright reproduced the Daisy & Fern opalescent pattern in blue, cranberry, and Vaseline. Some rose bowls in this pattern have Wright's squat, eight-crimped shape, and these are easy to identify. The spherical ones, however, have eight crimps, without the Fenton star, and resemble the originals in this pattern made by Northwood, West Virginia, and possibly Buckeye and Jefferson.

One way to tell them apart is color. This pattern was not originally made in Vaseline opalescent. All of those found in that color were made by Wright. Likewise, originals were not made with a matte finish. Those are also Wright. On the other hand, the originals also come in white opalescent, a color which Wright has not, to date, reproduced. So, the white ones are original.

Telling old from new is more difficult in glossy cranberry and blue, since both Wright and the original manufacturers made both of these colors. The design for Wright's Daisy & Fern seems to be a bit more "busy" than on the originals, though the copy is very good. This could just be a matter of individual perception, though on some pieces the foliage appears thicker on Wright's version.

The popular Wright Maize pattern rose bowls come only in the large size, making identification easy. When Libbey made this pattern at the turn of the century, it did not include crimped rose bowls, so all crimped Maize rose bowls were made by Wright. These date to the 1960s and 1970s. You can also distinguish Wright from Libbey Maize by color and casing. None of the original Libbey items were cased, while almost all Wright Maize is. Libbey Maize also features corn and foliage in different colors, where Wright pieces are all one color.

The Honeycomb pattern, which is sometimes found with the Fenton star, is a cranberry opalescent polka-dotted design. In the 1950s, Fenton did rose bowls and other shapes in a similar pattern, which it actually called "Polka Dot." Fenton and Wright's rose bowls in

Fig. 485. Wright did cased-overlay glass, much of which is decorated with florals in a number of colors. Wright overlay glass is found in both the spherical six-crimped shape and the larger squat shape. Author's collection.

Fig. 486. The cased blown-out rose design is another Wright pattern. Photo courtesy of Stu Horn.

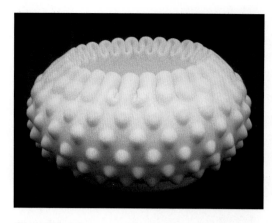

Fig. 487. Many people assume this shape in hobnail is Fenton, but it was actually in lines produced by both Fenton and Wright. Color and the number of crimps will probably prove to be the key in identification. Photo courtesy of Stu Horn.

Fig. 488. Crimped Daisy & Button rose bowls were all made by Wright and come in a variety of colors. Wright also produced a non-crimped version, which is sometimes found with a clear flower frog. Colors include amethyst, amber, amberina, green, and blue. Frosted treatments are also found. Photo courtesy of Stu Horn.

Fig. 491. Wright did its share of "Mary Gregory" designs, found in rose bowls as well as other shapes. With rose bowls, look for classic Wright shapes. Collection of Stu Horn.

Fig. 489. Daisy & Button rose bowls in purple and green. Author's collection.

Right: Fig. 490. The back of the Mary Gregory bowl.

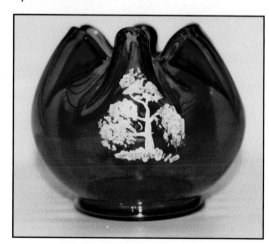

these patterns are easily identified because the colors are opposite. Wright's pattern is white with red spots. Fenton's is red with white spots. If you get the color schemes mixed up, don't worry. It's still easy to identify one from the other. Fenton's Polka Dot rose bowls have a band of white opalescence around the rim, extending to the bottom of the crimps. No such band appears on the Wright rose bowls. Instead, the dots extend right up to the crimps.

Wright made another cranberry opalescent pattern featuring circles, and they called it Eye Dot. Fenton's Coin Dot, made in the 1940s and 1950s, is similar, but the dots on the Fenton version are staggered. The circles on Wright's "Eye Dot" are aligned vertically.

Wright's peachblow line is also worth mentioning. It was primarily produced in the 1950s and 1960s, and is either pink with a white interior, or white with a pink interior. Fenton also had a peachblow line, which was white outside and pink inside. Rose bowls were made in both the large eight-crimped size, as well as the smaller spherical size, with both six and eight crimps. The eight-crimped versions bear the Fenton star and were apparently made by Fenton. Some of these items have a floral design known as Moss Rose painted on them.

Spherical rose bowls with eight crimps that do not bear the Fenton star were made in several additional patterns, including thumbprint, cranberry opalescent vertical stripe (called "rib" by the company), and Beaded Curtain, which comes in various cased colors, including peachblow. Beaded Curtain rose bowls were made in the 1940s and 1950s.

Of course, like Fenton, Wright has made rose bowls which do not fit the shapes discussed. Wright reproduced a Northwood opalescent pattern called Opal Open, beginning in the 1950s or 1960s. This rose bowl stands on a pedestal base with a circular decoration in the middle of the stem. In original Northwood pieces, the stem is open. In Wright pieces, the stem is solid. Wright's Opal Open rose bowls, which the company called "beaded ivy bowls," or "beaded open melon ivy bowls," are usually not opalescent, whereas Northwood's are. When in doubt, look at the stem, though, since this is a much better indicator than color.

Wright currently offers slag and opaque spatter glass rose bowls in a number of colors. These have eight crimps and rough pontils, and the glass is fairly thick. In addition, these do not have the collar foot found on every other Wright rose bowl, with the exception of Opal Open. The lack of foot and the rough pontil deviate totally from any of their earlier rose bowls.

Fig. 492. Since Wright is known to have acquired a number of Dugan molds, I believe this piece is Wright. Dugan is not known to have made this pattern in amberina, and the colors match those found in other pieces of Wright amberina. Collection of Stu Horn.

Fig. 493. Frank M. Fenton said he believes Fenton may have made these opalescent miniatures for Wright in the 1960s. It would make sense, since they have six crimps and a collar foot. 2-3/4" tall. Author's collection.

Fig. 494. Stand-alone of blue opalescent striped mini. Author's collection.

Fig. 495. Since Wright bought old Dugan molds, it would make sense that the company would duplicate a Dugan treatment. This miniature is nearly identical to larger Dugan bowls. Author's collection.

Left: Fig. 496. Wright produced rose bowls in the Priscilla pattern in a number of colors. Priscilla is a Victorian Dalzell pattern which was originally called Alexis. The original production was only in clear. Wright did both clear and colors. Author's collection.

3.2. Italian Reproductions of Victorian Art Glass

Satin and mother-of-pearl satin, Burmese, peachblow, nailsea, and spangled rose bowls were heavily reproduced by the Italians in the 1960s and 1970s. The Italians made many shapes in their line of art glass reproductions, and rose bowls are but one.

Italian reproduction rose bowls come in two sizes: a 3-inch version and a 5-inch version. Sometimes these copies can be found with stickers identifying their origin as Murano, an island off the Italian coast near Venice long renowned for glass making. Fortunately, stickers are not necessary for proper identification. These rose bowls can be identified through a number of characteristics, some of which are also shared by other shapes.

GLASS THICKNESS. Without a doubt, the glass on Italian reproductions is thicker than that found on original pieces of Victorian glass. Many times, reproduction glass is as much as 1/4-inch thick. In contrast, the glass on original pieces is often paper thin. Due to the thinness of the glass, original mother-of pearl items tend to bruise more easily than the newer examples.

THE "FEEL" OF THE GLASS. Original pieces with matte finishes are silky soft to the touch. In contrast, copies tend to have a gritty feel, which may have to do with differences in manufacturing. Although the exact process used by the Italians is unknown, it's quite possible their glass gets a matte finish from sandblasting, rather than from hydrofluoric acid. Many firms in the U.S. now rely on sandblasting instead of acid due to environmental laws. In any event, the difference is slight. To learn to recognize the subtle distinctions, examine—and handle—authentic pieces offered by a reputable dealer. Once you know what the real thing is supposed to feel like, it will be easier to notice the slight difference in the feel of the reproductions. Even if you're not planning to buy right away, don't be afraid to ask dealers to share their expertise. Most dealers of authentic Victorian glass are very willing to educate the public because educated collectors ultimately improve the market for them.

THE PONTILS. The pontils on authentic Victorian pieces vary considerably. However, the bottoms of reproductions are fairly consistent. Italian reproductions have what is best described as semi-ground pontils. Parts of the mark are rough, and other sections are ground smooth, or at least appear to have been. They look as if an attempt was made to grind them only so that the pieces would sit level.

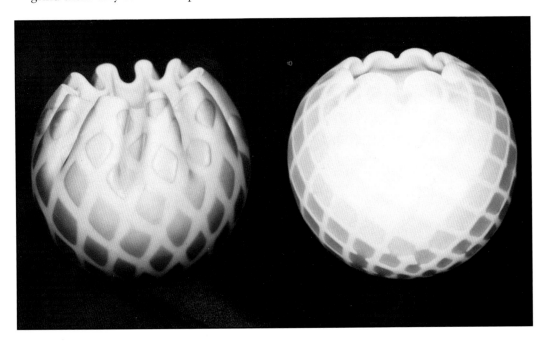

Fig. 497. Can you tell which one's real and which is Memorex? If you can't, you'd better read on! The green example is an Italian reproduction. The off-white example is Victorian Webb. Author's collection.

Fig. 499. These two are similar in overall shape, and even in the width of the lines making up the diamonds. But, if you compare the crimps and the shape of the diamonds, there really is no comparison. The green item is definitely Italian. The other is Webb. Author's collection.

Fig. 498. Note the thickness of the glass on this 3" Italian pink satin. The color change from pink to white is also rather abrupt. Author's collection.

Fig. 500. Italian rainbow mother-of-pearl is frequently mistaken for Victorian. Can you tell the difference? Look at the width of the lines making up the pattern, the crimp style, and the colors. Those on the authentic piece, left, are softer and more muted than on the Italian copy. Collection of Ruth Sparks.

Fig. 501. Look at this Italian copy of rainbow mother-of-pearl. Another clue to its origin is the thin dark line between yellow and blue. Collection of Frank B. Strovel, Jr.

Fig. 502. A selection of Italian mother-of-pearl diamond-quilted rose bowls. Collections of author and Stu Horn.

Fig. 503. More Italian diamond quilted mother-of-pearl rose bowls. Collections of author and Stu Horn.

Fig. 504. Beware of unusual colors in mother-of-pearl satin. This large bowl is Italian. The diamonds are elongated, and it has five uneven crimps, in addition to a rough pontil. Author's collection.

Fig. 505. Italian reproduction rose bowls are quite nice in their own way. This slightly squat example has lovely coloring. The width of the lines making up the pattern, the stark white lining and pontil give away it's relative lack of age. Collection of Stu Horn.

SHAPE. Italian copies tend to be rather long and egg shaped, although this shape is less noticeable in the larger size rose bowls than in the smaller ones. The widest portion of the bowl will be just below the center.

Another typical Italian reproduction shape, found most often in mother-of pearl glass, is a squat rose bowl on three frosted toes. This form imitates the shapes often found in English glass by famous firms such as Thomas Webb, and Stevens & Williams. However, authentic pieces in this shape are seldom made of mother-of-pearl glass. That's not to say they don't exist. Just beware. Applied glass toes are also found in both clear and frosted on originals, but are usually frosted only on reproductions. If in doubt, look for a gritty feel to the glass, a half-ground pontil, or a lopsided prunt covering the pontil. Sometimes the pieces themselves are lopsided, with one side sitting slightly lower than the other.

CRIMP STYLE. Where the elongated shape leaves off, crimp style takes over as a means of identification. On rose bowls, as well as baskets, toothpicks, and many styles of vases, Italian crimps look as if they were pinched, like a cook would pinch pie crust to make the fluted edges. The crimps are frequently uneven, and pointed or a bit square. In contrast, authentic crimps flow into one another and are softly rounded.

In addition, Italian rose bowls can be found with anywhere from five to twelve crimps. Authentic pieces generally have an even number of crimps, usually six, eight, or twelve. If you find one with five, seven, nine, or eleven, beware! The exception to this rule (isn't there always an exception?) is Libbey's 1893 World's Fair peachblow rose bowls. These were intended to be inexpensive souvenir pieces, so

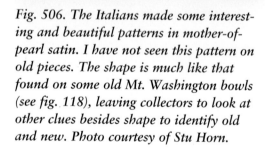

Fig. 506. *The Italians made some interesting and beautiful patterns in mother-of-pearl satin. I have not seen this pattern on old pieces. The shape is much like that found on some old Mt. Washington bowls (see fig. 118), leaving collectors to look at other clues besides shape to identify old and new. Photo courtesy of Stu Horn.*

Fig. 507. *This is a quite lovely example with rich green coloring and applied glass feet. But, it is still Italian. If you look closely you will see that the shape is slightly lopsided, something you will seldom find on Victorian examples. The elongated diamonds, stark white lining, and rough pontil also give it away. Author's collection.*

Fig. 508. That's Italian! Don't be fooled. Even author William Heacock says he was fooled the first time he saw an example like this. This shape and glass treatment is shown in AA Importing catalogs from the 1960s. Photo courtesy of Stu Horn.

Fig. 509. The Italians copied spatter glass and made rose bowls, though these are not nearly as common as their mother-of-pearl satin cousins. Note the crimp style. If you're having trouble focusing, it's not you, it's the bowl, which has a matte finish and looks a bit out of focus! You won't find this on old spatter glass. Collection of David Billings.

Fig. 510. The shape and crimp style give away the Italian identity of this Nailsea rose bowl. Photo courtesy of Stu Horn.

less attention was paid to quality than with Libbey's regular lines. Mt. Washington rose bowls also typically have nine crimps. If in doubt, consider all the characteristics of the glass, not just the number of crimps.

COLOR. Burmese and peachblow reproductions are easily identified by color. Authentic Burmese shades from a rose pink to golden yellow. Some of the reproduction Italian Burmese items have good color, but often the colors appear rather drab in comparison to those found on original pieces. The main type of peachblow to be reproduced by the Italians is Mt. Washington, which shades from a delicate rose pink to powder blue gray. Reproductions have poor color, being much darker, and they are often characterized by a band of purple dividing the two colors. This band is not found on originals.

With rose bowls, remember that size does count. Thomas Webb made the Victorian Burmese rose bowls 3 inches tall and in smaller sizes, making a 5-inch Burmese rose bowl suspect from the start. With a 3-inch Burmese rose bowl, consider crimp style, the pontil, the feel of the glass, and color.

Reproductions of both Burmese and peachblow often change color quickly, where the colors on authentic pieces simply fade into one another almost imperceptibly. Mt. Washington peachblow looks like the colors were created by pink and blue-gray powder dusted on the piece from opposite ends until they met in the middle. This soft coloration is not found on copies. In addition, you will often see striations of each color throughout reproduction pieces. With Burmese, for example, pontils often look like marbled, with both pink and yellow visible. Authentic pieces will have no such striations.

Fig. 511. A selection of Italian Burmese rose bowls in both sizes, with one example of the less-common "peachblow" copy (back, right.) Author's and Stu Horn's collections.

Fig. 512. Pigeon blood Aventurine. Collection of Frank B. Strovel, Jr.

Fig. 513. The Italians made "Aventurine" rose bowls with a pulled-feather design in both green and pigeon blood. Don't be fooled. Look at the crimps, glass thickness and pontils, and compare them to known Italian shapes. I have never seen an old rose bowl with this treatment. I have seen these with fake Quezal signatures. Quezal did not make crimped rose bowls. Collection of Stu Horn.

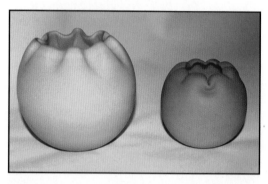

Fig. 514. Can you tell authentic Burmese from 1960s Italian Burmese rose bowls? Pay attention to differences in color, size, shape, and crimp style. Spotting the real thing here (it's the tiny one on the right) is a bit tough because it apparently is a second. Author's collection.

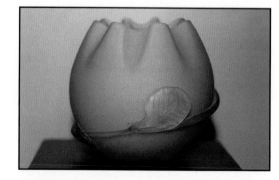

Fig. 515. Note how washed out the colors are on this Burmese example. And, the applied foliage spirals in a straight line around the piece. Applied foliage on Victorian pieces bends and turns like real foliage. Photo courtesy of Harriet Clough.

Satin reproductions are not particularly common and pink is the main color to show up. It is often very dark pink at the top, and nearly white almost immediately below the crimps. Blue is the most commonly found color in reproduction mother-of pearl, while yellow is the most common authentic color to be found, at least in rose bowls. The Italian yellow is considerably brighter than authentic yellow, but the Italian blue and pink colors are very close to colors found on old pieces. You will also find reproduction mother-of pearl in many unusual colors, such as royal blue, green, orange, and rainbow, which are colors rarely seen in authentic mother-of pearl. Authentic rainbow pieces, when they do show up on the market, are characterized by very soft, muted colors. Reproductions, in contrast, have well-defined colors, and sometimes a definite line divides one color from the next.

Italian Nailsea is most often found in white or off-white, with reddish orange loops. This color is not known in authentic Nailsea pieces. The pattern is also found in blue.

PATTERN. Mother-of pearl satin glass is the most prolific of the Italian reproductions, especially in the diamond-quilted pattern. Although other patterns were made, it seems that only herringbone shows up with any frequency. But collectors must still be aware that other patterns were produced.

The diamonds on Italian reproduction diamond-quilted mother-of pearl glass tend to be larger than those found on authentic pieces. They are often also somewhat elongated, compared to originals which are wider and more square. The lines that make up the patterns are generally considerably wider on reproductions than on originals.

With Italian Nailsea, there are far fewer loops on a single piece than is generally found on authentic pieces. Usually the loops are spaced far apart, in contrast to rather closely spaced loops on originals.

DECORATION. Italian reproductions are seldom decorated with painted or enameled designs, though a Mary Gregory-type decoration can sometimes be found on Burmese rose

Fig. 516. OK, quiz time! Can you tell which is authentic and which is Italian? It should be easy, since you've seen the green Italian item before. But notice how thick the glass is on the authentic rose version. This just proves that one characteristic alone is not enough to properly identify any piece. Author's collection.

Fig. 517. *This quiz should be a little tougher than the one on the last page. The crimps, lining color, and slightly lopsided shape of the larger Italian copy make it obvious to those who have studied reproductions. Author's collection.*

bowls, and possibly on other types of glass as well. Italian pieces are more likely to be decorated with applied glass. Petal feet and handles, usually in frosted glass, are rather common. When applied glass foliage appears on the body of the piece, it spirals around the piece, counterclockwise from bottom to top, and the stems are very straight. Authentic applied glass foliage is not straight, but more random—like a real tree branch or stem would be.

Of course, it's important to note that no single characteristic guarantees that a piece is old or new. Sometimes, for example, authentic mother-of-pearl glass can be rather thick. In such a case, it is important to examine the piece for other characteristics, such as the feel of the glass, the pontil, and the decoration. All characteristics considered together will provide the big picture and lead the collector to a proper identification.

Fig. 518. *An easy way to tell if this is Victorian or Italian is to look at the color. Rose bowls were ever made in authentic Victorian plated amberina. Author's collection.*

Italian reproductions are beautiful and collectible in their own right. And, when they first appeared on the retail market, they were sold for what they actually were—reproductions. Today, however, they're hitting the secondary market in large enough numbers to cause real confusion. Some dealers may honestly not know the difference, while some may not even care to know. Regardless, few sellers offer them as the reproductions that they are. It's up to you, the buyer, to know whether what is being offered is an original or a reproduction.

3.3. Italian Originals

In addition to the reproductions, the Italians made rose bowls in a variety of other types of glass. Among them are translucent pink or blue glass with applied glass decorations, latticino, and millefiore (both with a solid color background and a few canes of millefiore throughout, with an all-over millefiore design). I call these "originals" because rose bowls were not originally made in these types of glass, with the possible exception of all-over millefiore. Most millefiore rose bowls are late models, however.

It's quite possible that additional styles and designs were also produced. Look for the telltale Italian shape, pontil, and crimp style. These characteristics are consistent with 1960s and 1970s Italian rose bowls no matter what their style.

In addition to the opaque styles discussed above, the Italians made some nice blown transparent glass rose bowls with applied rigaree. These are shaped very differently from those discussed above. They have completely rough pontils, are much more spherical in shape, and have eight generally even crimps. The crimps are shallow, kind of like Mt. Washington's or Webb's, but not quite of that high quality. And the colors are wonderful! I've seen a wonderful ruby and Caribbean blue, lavender, pink, green, and amber, and some with threaded designs.

Fig. 519. Latticino rose bowl, c. 1973. Crimped rose bowls are not found in older latticino. Author's collection.

The main characteristic to look for here is the applied rigaree around the bottom, though some examples also have a band of rigaree around the centers, like a ring around Saturn. This rigaree can also help identify later pieces of millefiore and latticino, though not all pieces from this era have the rigaree.

Of course, the Italians are well known for latticino and heavy paperweight-style glass items, and rose bowls are sometimes found in these styles, too.

Fig. 520. Non-crimped latticino rose bowl. The applied rigaree base indicates it was also made in the 1960s. Photo courtesy of Stu Horn.

*Fig. 521. A selection of Italian originals
in various colors, with the telltale applied
rigaree decorations. Collections of the
author and Stu Horn.*

*Fig. 522. Paperweight-style rose bowl made in Murano. Exact age
undetermined, but the stickers appearing on these examples are
similar to stickers used in the 1960s. Collection of Stu Horn.*

Fig. 523. Large stemmed Italian rose bowl, standing 11-1/2" tall. These can be found in other colors and shape variations, all with the swag treatment and medallion stem. Author's collection.

3.4. Japanese Reproductions of Satin and Spangled Glass

These copies, which came to the U.S. during the late 1970s and into the 1980s, share many of the same characteristics as their Italian cousins. The main differences between these and the Italian reproductions are shape, crimp style, and pontils.

The Japanese copies, which I have seen in yellow, blue, pink, orange, and lavender satin, and in at least as many colors in spangled glass, are wider and rounder than the Italian versions. Some, in fact, are perfectly spherical like their Victorian counterparts, though these are relatively few. For the most part, they tend to be kind of square and boxy, with tall crimps that point slightly outward.

The bottoms of these pieces are also quite different. Instead of a rough pontil, they have no pontil at all. The bottoms are flat, and smooth as a table top. Occasionally, however, there will be a rough pontil indented from the rest of the table-top smooth bottom (see fig. 528).

In addition to satin and spangled glass, watch for a pseudo-cameo in this shape, and a translucent reddish version which is somewhat smaller than those made in satin and spangled glass.

Following is known catalog information for Japanese rose bowls sold by AA Importing of St. Louis. Please note this is not a complete list, since many additional shapes and colors are known.

O/2903V or O/2903B—"Daisy and Button," 7" with opalescent rim. Vaseline or Blue. $6.75 each. Available 1973. (one panel with design, the rest plain and ribbed.)

IA/2109—Ribbon glass, available 1973.

CO271—Cobalt overlay, available 1950-present.

CO272—Same as above in ruby, available 1950-present.

JA1856B—Blue satin, available in the late 1970s and early 1980s.

JA1865Y—Same as above in yellow, available late 1970s and early 1980s. Other colors seen on the market include pink, orange, and lavender.

JA1854—Cranberry thumbprint, also available in the 1980s.

JA1830—Ruby cut to clear, dot pattern, Thousand-Eye Rose Bowl, 4-1/2" across, crimped rim, $4.50 each, available late 1970s and early 1980s.

JA1813—"Opal dot," white opalescent/dot pattern, available late 1970s, early 1980s.

 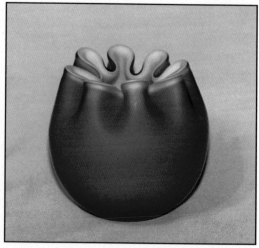

Fig. 524. Japanese lavender satin. These are also found in blue, pink, yellow, and orange, with other colors possible. Note the lack of shading, glass thickness, and crimp style. Collection of Stu Horn.

Fig. 525. Japanese pink satin. Pay particular attention to the similarity in its shape and the shapes of figs. 527 and 529. Photo courtesy of Emily Minton.

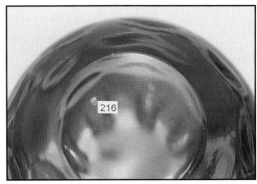

Fig. 526. The bottoms of most Japanese rose bowls are table-top smooth.

Left: Fig. 527. Lovely Japanese cranberry example. Author's collection.

Fig. 528. If there is a pontil at all, it looks like a little belly button indentation on an otherwise table-top smooth bottom. This is the bottom of the item in fig. 529.

Fig. 529. This reddish example is somewhat smaller than other Japanese late models. These have been seen with forged "Steuben" signatures. Author's collection.

Fig. 530. Cut-to-clear pattern, available in 1970s and 1980s. Collection of Stu Horn.

Figs. 531 and 532. These rose-cut overlay rose bowls have been imported into this country since at least the 1950s, and are still available on the wholesale and retail market. A grape pattern was also produced in these colors, but has not been imported for nearly as long and is not found as often on the secondary market.

3.5. American Peachblow and Burmese Reproductions

A line of reproductions of New England peachblow, which includes a rose bowl, was made in the late 1960s by Harold Bennett, of the Guernsey Glass Co., Inc., in Cambridge, Ohio. These were originally signed "BENNETT" in script, but these signatures have been ground off the vast majority of the rose bowls.

Although these items were made using the original New England formula, the trained eye can easily spot the newer pieces. They look a lot like unlined pink satin glass, and the crimps are turned in and often a bit "smooshed." The shape is definitely not as nice as those found in regular pink satin glass.

A second American reproduction of peachblow, and Burmese for that matter, was made by Intaglio, of Alton, Illinois. Although the line is called "Mimosa," the company's 1993 ads read, "More commonly known as peachblow." Intaglio's peachblow shades from pink to white, and often has a lattice pattern. The rose bowl in this line has three crimps and is quite heavy. It also appears in Burmese, although I do not know how old the Burmese is. Intaglio is run by Gary W. Levi, who ran Levay in the 1980s, so it is not particularly old.

Incidentally, an Intaglio ad in the June/July 1994 issue of *Glass Collector's Digest* shows several rose bowls in iridescent and other treatments. These are bound to show up soon on the secondary market and be mistaken for other things.

Wright and Fenton also produced "peachblow" lines, which are discussed in sections 3.1 and 3.6. Other companies also had lines known as "peachblow," but these are not known to have included rose bowls.

Fig. 533. This version of unlined pink satin glass is likely to have been part of the Harold Bennett line of peachblow from the 1960s. Collection of David Billings.

3.6. Fenton's Late Models

Although Fenton has been making rose bowls since its founding, the vast majority of Fenton rose bowls fit into this time period. Frank M. Fenton says that rose bowls have traditionally been a tough sell for the company. It's not that they don't sell; it's just that other shapes in the same line as the rose bowls sell better. This doesn't seem to be too much of a problem for the company, however, since it has made rose bowls in abundance during the last forty years.

Before getting into Fenton's line, I should explain the term "satin," as it is used by Fenton and other companies. As discussed in section 1.1, satin glass is a type of Victorian art glass that is given a satin finish through a bath in hydrofluoric acid. Knowing that, it is confusing for some to see what might be called "frosted glass" being advertised as "satin." To some, the term "satin glass" means that the piece has a matte finish. This is not entirely correct, since transparent glass can have a matte finish and still not be satin glass. It would be more correctly described as "frosted."

On the other hand, companies such as Fenton have used the term "satin" to refer to items in their line that have a matte finish. I believe they even have a color called cameo satin, which is a brown opalescent and does not even necessarily have a matte finish. Nor is it anything like the type of glass called cameo. Although neither "cameo" nor "satin" are correct from a Victorian art glass perspective, the terminology is not incorrect when referring to this particular Fenton color. Since companies seem to recycle terms like "satin" and "cameo," it's important for collectors to understand that all items described with these terms are not created equal.

Among Fenton's most famous and collectible lines is their Burmese, which includes several rose bowls. First introduced in 1970, Fenton's version of this heat-sensitive glass tends to be brighter and more yellow than the Burmese made a century ago. Striations of both colors are often found throughout the piece, rather than a gradual switch from one hue to the other. Once you know what Fenton Burmese looks like, you'll have no trouble identifying it.

Fenton made Burmese rose bowls in its typical 3-1/2-inch size, but also made them in a squat miniature and in embossed shapes such as Lily of the Valley and Poppy. The first rose

Fig. 534. Leaf Decorated Burmese was the first of Fenton's Burmese designs to be made in rose bowls. They date from 1970 to 1972. Author's collection.

Fig. 535. Mary Walrath's Love Bouquet miniature rose bowls were limited to 650 pieces, and were made in 1986. A spherical "cupped" rose bowl was also made in this design. Author's collection.

Fig. 537. A special limited edition Burmese "Circle of Love" rose bowl made for Joyce Colella. This one is #55 of 80 made in 1997. Author's collection.

Fig. 536. The Burmese Poppy rose bowl was sold on QVC in 1997.

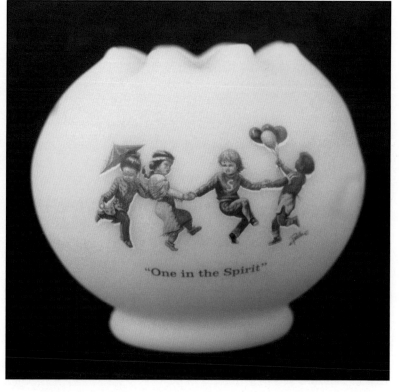

Figs. 538 and 539. Fenton custard "One in the Spirit" rose bowl sample done for Mary Walrath and her daughter Carol Wood. Author's collection.

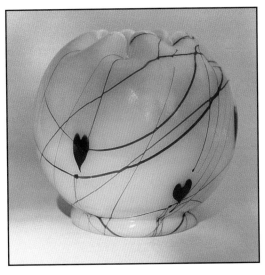

Fig. 540. Robert Barber Hanging Hearts rose bowl, c. 1976. Collection of Frank B. Strovel, Jr.

Fig. 541. Turquoise Hanging Hearts. Collection of Stu Horn.

bowls to appear in Fenton Burmese were undecorated 3-1/2-inch blanks, which perfectly exhibit the Fenton shape discussed in the last chapter. In addition to the eight-crimped versions are similarly shaped rose bowls with about thirty tightly pleated crimps. This version is usually found undecorated.

Next to appear was the Leaf Decorated Burmese rose bowl, made from 1970 to 1972. Rose bowls are also plentiful in rose-decorated Burmese, which is the first hand-painted Fenton Burmese, developed by decorator Louise Piper in 1971. You'll also find scenic decorated rose bowls, produced between 1973 and 1979. A few other decorations also exist, but these are relatively scarce.

Fenton's rose bowl shapes in Burmese broadened in the 1980s with the introduction of Mary Walrath's Cherished Editions in 1982. The Love Bouquet pattern, featuring roses and lily of the valley, came in both a cupped (typical Fenton shape) and a squat miniature. These are also found undecorated.

Though perhaps not as famous as Burmese, Fenton's Robert Barber rose bowls are more stunning. Barber, who worked at Fenton in 1976, created a blue and white looped "Cascade Vase" in a rose bowl shape. He also produced rose bowls in turquoise and custard in the hanging hearts pattern. All of these were limited editions.

The limited edition Cascade Vases came in a glossy finish, but a few can be found with a matte finish. According to Mr. Fenton, these were seconds, given a matte finish and sold in the factory gift shop. It's hard for me to believe that such a stunning piece from my own collection (depicted on this book's cover) is a second! It attracts attention and positive comments from nearly everyone who comes to visit, glass lover or not. I don't know how many seconds exist. The firsts were limited to 700 pieces.

Additional Fenton rose bowls will be discussed in the photo captions.

Fig. 542. Fenton Fine Dot rose bowls, made in the 1950s and 1960s, have an inverted hobnail pattern. They're also found in Vaseline and cranberry opalescent, but the opalescent colors are later production. Author's collection.

 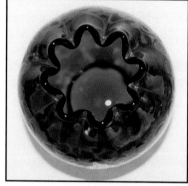

Figs. 544 and 545. Fine Dot rose bowls provide good examples of the Fenton Star.

Fig. 546. Fenton used the same squat shape as in the Mary Walrath Love Bouquet line to make souvenirs for a Fenton Art Glass collectors convention. Author's collection.

Fig. 543. The Beatty Honeycomb rose bowl is one of only two Fenton rose bowls lacking some kind of foot or toes. Beatty did not make crimped items in its Honeycomb pattern.

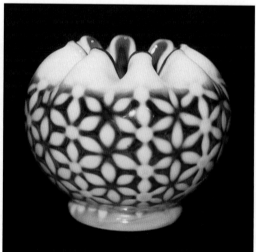

Fig. 547. The Fenton snowflake pattern rose bowl is recent, since it is marked. Wright also made a snowflake pattern, usually found in its large, squat shape. Collection of Stu Horn.

Fig. 548. Fenton's version of Northwood's Drapery pattern is found with three toes, rather than a collar foot. Those with looped handles were made by Fenton for Levay in the 1980s.

Fig. 549. Fenton made toed egg-shaped hobnail rose bowls, with no opalescence, in a variety of colors in the 1960s. Courtesy of Grandma Patty's Antiques.

Fig. 550. The Poppy pattern comes in a variety of glass treatments. The cranberry example has been available on the retail market for some time. The blue version is a little older, though the exact age is unknown. Collection of Stu Horn.

Left: Fig. 551. This item appears to be Bohemian at first glance, but it is actually a Fenton rose bowl from the 1980s. Courtesy of Grandma Patty's Antiques.

Fig. 553. Fenton's Plum Carnival rose bowl, sold on QVC in 1995. Author's Collection.

Fig. 552. This decorated amethyst rose bowl was sold on QVC in 1998 to celebrate Bill Fenton's 75th birthday. Author's collection.

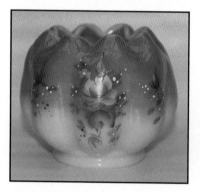

Fig. 554. This Fenton Rosalene rose bowl was sold on QVC in the early 1990s. Collection of Stu Horn.

Fig. 555. Colored overlay rose bowls are in the current line, and are found with various floral decorations. They're sometimes found with six crimps, too, so don't assume that this shape with six crimps is Wright. Collection of Stu Horn.

Fig. 556. Fenton's Lily of the Valley pattern rose bowls have been in the line since the 1980s, and are found in a number of colors.

Figs. 557-558. Decorator Marilyn Wagner acquired some amethyst blanks and did her own decorations. This Wild Horses design is one of only three known. The photo on the left shows the back. The design goes the whole way around the bowl. Author's collection.

Fig. 559. One of a number of "pattern glass" rose bowls Fenton currently offers. Westmoreland is also producing similar rose bowls.

Fig. 560. Unicorns were another subject chosen by Ms. Wagner, and only a handful are known to exist. Collection of Stu Horn.

3.7. Miscellaneous Late Models

Glass companies along the Ohio River have made rose bowls in limited quantities over the past forty years. Blenko, located in Milton, West Virginia, made free-blown versions with thirty tight crimps. They also made crackle glass rose bowls which are difficult to distinguish from those made at their competitors' factories. One competitor, Pilgrim Glass of Ceredo, West Virginia, still makes crackle rose bowls in cranberry and cobalt.

A few rose bowls continue to come out of Europe, but many of these are not crimped. Aside from the Italians, the Japanese, and Fenton, production of crimped rose bowls is definitely proceeding at a much slower pace than it did a century ago.

Still, quantity is not always what's important. I have included photos of two special custom-made rose bowls, the likes of which you won't see again unless you know their owners. I felt these were worth including, not only because you will have a chance to see something you might not otherwise see, but also because it illustrates the passion with which rose bowl collectors go about their hobby.

Fig. 561. This cut bowl has a Czech-style design. Because of the style of cutting, it is believed to be a late model. Late model cut glass rose bowls often have some cuts that are not polished. Photo courtesy of Rose Beach.

Fig. 562. In recent years, the Czechs also made uncrimped hobnail rose bowls in a number of colors and glass treatments. Photo courtesy of Stu Horn.

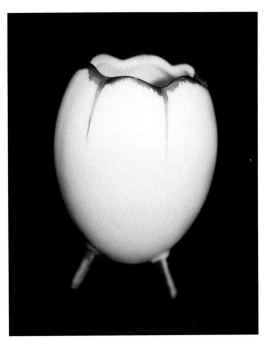

Fig. 563. Lefton china miniature egg-style rose bowl. The intended purpose for this piece is uncertain, but it works well with a rose bowl collection. Measuring 2-5/8" tall, it came with a matching under plate. Author's collection.

Fig. 564. The age of this china example is unknown, but I estimate it to be fairly recent. The signature appears to read, "Diane Art Studio PLAT." The silver highlights are actually platinum. It measures 1-3/4" high. Author's collection.

Fig. 565. Belleek in a rose bowl shape. It has a green mark which includes a small "r" above the right end of the ribbon, indicating that it dates from 1956 to 1965.

Fig. 566. This earthenware Gibson's Staffordshire bowl dates from 1930 to 1972, according to the mark. Author's collection.

Fig. 567. Limoges rose bowl. The mark dates it to 1970 and later. Collection of Martha Ross.

Fig. 568. Colored milk glass rose bowls are found in green, blue, amethyst, and smoke. They have visible mold marks, but the age and origins are unknown. Collection of Martha Ross.

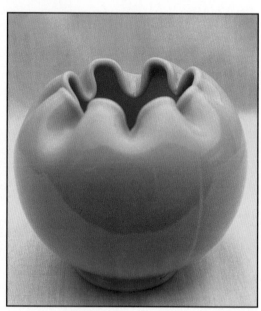

Fig. 569. Green milk glass. Author's collection.

Fig. 570. An example of 1960s Carnival, by Imperial. The finish is glossy and unworn. The mark, an "I" over a "G," was used from 1951 to 1972. Author's collection.

Fig. 571. Blenko rose bowls are free-blown and have rough pontils.

Fig. 572. Imperial also re-introduced its Molly pattern. Author's collection.

Fig. 573. This mark is the same as that on the piece shown in fig. 570, except that it has an "L" in front of it, indicating that the bowl was made from 1973 to 1981.

Fig. 574. Close-up of amethyst Blenko.

Fig. 575. Blenko, which is still in business in Milton, West Virginia, made rose bowls with thirty pleated crimps, c. 1952. They're found in amethyst, ruby, orange, amber, clear, and two shades of green. Rough pontils. Author's collection.

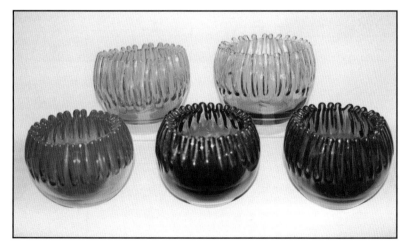

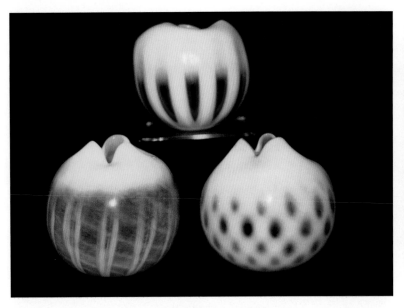

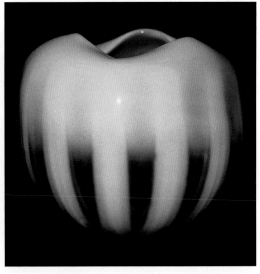

Fig. 576. Intaglio, of Alton, Illinois, made these heavy opalescent three-crimped examples. Company owner Gary Levi says his niece calls them "fish lips." Appropriate! Rough pontils. Author's and Stu Horn's collections.

Fig. 577. This example doesn't have the fish lips, but based on the other characteristics of the glass, an Intaglio attribution is in order.

Fig. 578. Crackle glass rose bowls were made in a variety of colors by Blenko, Pilgrim, and possibly others, from the 1950s on. Pilgrim still makes them in cranberry and cobalt. Collection of Martha Ross.

Fig. 579. Westmoreland's English Hobnail rose bowls come both stemmed and unfooted. However, iridized versions were made by Plum Glass of Pittsburgh, Pennsylvania. Collection of Frank B. Strovel, Jr.

Fig. 580. Pairpoint paper label.

Fig. 581. Pairpoint, successor to Mt. Washington Glass, is still in business. This whimsy was purchased from the factory showroom in 1998. Author's collection.

Fig. 582. This might not be the oldest, or even the most valuable rose bowl in Ruth Sparks' collection, but it is the most special. Her late husband George had it custom made for her at Pairpoint in 1975.

Figs. 583 and 584. Martha Ross also has a custom-made example in her collection. She had it made for her Victorian doll house. (It's on top of the bowfront on the left side of the room).

3.8. Signatures

Don't believe everything you read. Since fake signatures are a troublesome element in glass, and are often found on late model rose bowls, I felt this was the proper place for an in-depth discussion.

Few things evoke more emotion in glass collectors than signatures. Right or wrong, most collectors will pay more for a signed piece than an unsigned one. Beginning collectors often make the mistake of accepting a signature as proof of a piece's authenticity, while at the same time questioning the authenticity of pieces that aren't signed.

In my experience, far more rose bowls are unsigned than signed. Still, when you find one that is signed, you shouldn't necessarily take the signature as proof positive of a particular identification. Why? First and foremost because fake signatures are being applied to both authentic pieces and copies faster than collectors can acquire new rose bowls—and that's pretty fast!

The first time I encountered a fake signature on a rose bowl was when a member of the Rose Bowl Collectors Club contacted me about his translucent reddish-rose-colored one with a Steuben fleur de lis signature. Since the rose bowl was obviously a recent import, the signature had to be a fake. Fortunately, this person buys what he likes, and did not buy the piece because he thought it was an authentic Steuben.

Fake Steuben fleur de lis signatures are among the most prolific of the forgeries, turning up on many pieces which in no way, shape or form—and this is meant quite literally—are Steuben. To accurately identify Steuben, as with any type of glass, you must consider factors such as shape, pattern, and color before looking for a signature.

Steuben is not the only name to be plagued by forged signatures. I have encountered rose bowls with the acid stamped letters "S&W." I imagine this was supposed to be a Stevens & Williams signature. However, the piece was obviously an Italian reproduction from the 1960s. Besides, the British company never signed its wares this way. To see what authentic Stevens & Williams signatures look like, I recommend referring to a copy of *British Glass: 1800-1914*, by Charles R. Hajdamach. There are far too many signatures to even attempt to describe them all here.

Interestingly, Frederick Carder, who worked for Stevens & Williams before moving to America and working for Steuben, is not nearly so well thought of in the U.K. as he is in America. In fact, Carder is seen by some as an opportunist who brought ideas, techniques, and forms from his former employer, Stevens & Williams, to America, where he pawned them off as his own.

"In America, unlike England, the name of Frederick Carder is held in total reverence," writes Hajdamach. "Any serious questioning of Carder myths is rarely expressed in public, a situation which makes it ideal for the forger to produce 'Carder/Stevens & Williams' fakes."

But fake signatures don't end with pieces associated with Carder. At a large antiques and collectibles show, I saw a pink mother-of-pearl satin beverage set acid stamped "WEBB." I admit that I was perplexed by the signature at first. However, I have since done some research, and found out that this signature is also a forgery. In fact, there are three British companies with "Webb" as part of their names: Thomas Webb & Sons, Webb-Corbett, and Webb Richardson. They would have no reason to sign a piece simply as "Webb," since it could be mistaken for a product of one of the other firms.

Authentic Webb signatures also appear in *British Glass*, as do Stevens & Williams registry numbers which are found on Jewell Glass and other lines.

Fake Galle cameo pieces also often carry signatures. Romanian-made copies will often carry the mark "tip," which is the Romanian word for "type," says the June 1994 issue of *Antique & Collectors Reproduction News*. The word was used to avoid legal troubles with those who claim the rights to the name Galle, so it is not necessarily found on all Galle reproductions, and sometimes it is ground off.

Of course, the abundance of fake Galle doesn't really affect rose bowl collectors all that much, since no known Galle rose bowls exist. But you should be aware that forgeries do exist for virtually every signature and mark out there.

The second reason to avoid using signatures as proof of authenticity is their inconsistent use. Steuben did not mark all of its products. Nor did many other companies. In a discussion of Pairpoint lamps at a Mt. Washington Art Glass Society convention, for instance, noted Mt. Washington/Pairpoint scholar Louis O. St. Aubin Jr. noted that some of the glass lampshades are signed, but these are not necessarily examples of the artists' or the company's best work. On QVC, Bill Fenton often explains that although Fenton began using signatures in the early 1970s, some pieces will still escape without the Fenton mark due to mold wear or other factors. Many times, when a signature is present, it is very faint. In addition to attribution, this clouds the issue of age, since an unmarked piece of Fenton can still be brand new. Many companies marked their pieces with nothing more than paper labels, most of which were lost.

An unfortunate byproduct of our signature-crazy thinking is that many unsigned pieces are inaccurately attributed. An amethyst intaglio-cut rose bowl shown in this book is marked "Moser Karlsbad." But the Harrach firm did similar work. So, all intaglio-cut pieces like this one are not necessarily Moser. An unsigned piece could just as easily be Harrach as Moser. Likewise, I have seen many Rossler rose bowls incorrectly represented as Moser.

On the flip side, sometimes the lack of a signature has a significant meaning not necessarily related to authenticity. In the case of Swedish maker Orrefors, for example, seconds were not signed. These seconds were sold with green paper labels. The value of such pieces is dramatically less than that of a signed piece, however. That didn't stop at least one person from trying to sign, albeit crudely, an Orrefors second with their "Of" signature!

The last word here is not to get too caught up in the presence or absence of a signature. Many quality pieces are unsigned. Many signed pieces are fakes. The best advice I can give to any collector is to look at the glass itself. Is the color, form, shape, and feel of the glass consistent with that of a particular maker? Look at the signature last, and use it as evidence of authenticity only if all the other qualities of the glass hold up. And, if there's no signature, by all means, don't sweat it!

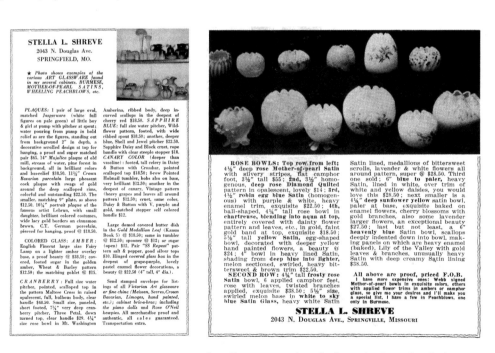

Fig. 585. Some vintage antique ads offering rose bowls for sale. Imagine being able to go back in time to the 1950s, when these Spinning Wheel ads ran, and buy rose bowls at these prices!

182 Collectible Glass Rose Bowls

rose bowl
PRICE GUIDE

It has been written before, and I'll write it once again here: This price list is intended to be used only as a guide and not as gospel or proof of any item's value.

Because prices vary from region to region, and according to buyer taste, I have created ranges for most of the rose bowls listed. The lower end of the range would be for the East Coast, where prices for glass generally seem to be lowest, or for rose bowls in a particular category which fall at the lower end of the spectrum in terms of quality, scarcity, or desirability. The higher end of the range would apply to other parts of the country, where prices tend to be higher, or for more scarce and/or desirable pieces in that same category. For example, under Shell Embossed, I list the range for all colors. You would, therefore, expect to pay around $125 for a yellow rose bowl, and closer to $175 for the unusual white decorated rose bowl.

The prices quoted here are for retail buying, with no "dealer discount." In order to come up with the prices, I have relied on data gathered over the past several years from a variety of sources including auctions, shows, shops, and private sales. This process has provided more than enough data to price the more common examples. However, with rare colors or unusual patterns, I had very little data to go on. That is the pitfall of including a number of rare and unusual examples that you just don't see every day.

I turned to price guides compiled by others. Unfortunately, they usually didn't have a price for the exact piece I was looking for. As a result, I had to go with my best estimate, based on my long-term experience and knowledge of what I have seen other shapes in these treatments selling for. Unlike Depression or Carnival glass, where a series of known shapes and patterns exists, there is no end to the variety of rose bowls found. (And prices vary so much by color in Carnival, that this created another logistical nightmare!) There's simply no way to price all of the rose bowls with any accuracy. In some cases, I chose not to price a particular piece at all. I would rather not price it than to pull a number out of the air and mislead everyone.

Which brings me back to my opening statement: This price guide is intended only as a guide. Consider the prices listed here as one resource that, combined with your own experience and intuition, will assist you in coming up with an appropriate value for the piece that you are selling or considering purchasing.

1.1. Satin and Mother-of-Pearl Satin

Undecorated satins—pink, blue, yellow (fig. 4) . . . . $65-$85

Undecorated "glossy" satin—pink, blue, yellow (fig. 5) . . . . $55-$75

Undecorated satins—purple, green, etc. (figs. 7-10) . . . . $75-$125

Undecorated satins, egg style—pink, blue, yellow (fig. 68, right) . . . . $40-$70

Undecorated satins, egg style, "glossy" (fig. 67) . . . . $40-$70

Undecorated satins, unusual shapes (figs. 6, 58) . . . . $90-$150

Enamel decorated satins—pink, blue, yellow (figs. 13-15, 19, 21) . . . . . . $95-$150

Enamel decorated satins—purple, green, etc. (figs. 12, 16-18, 20, 22, 366) . . . .
. . . . $110-$175

Decorated satins, egg style—pink, blue, yellow (figs. 68, left, 65, 66) . . . $75-$110

Satins, cottage, unfired decorations (figs. 368-370) . . . . $65-$75

Glossy enameled—pink, blue, yellow (fig. 25) . . . . $65-$95

Fan Embossed—raspberry, custard, turquoise (figs. 23, 24, 26) . . . . $40-$75

Cabbage Rose—pink, blue, yellow (fig. 28) . . . . $100-$150

Cabbage Rose—purple, green (figs. 27, 30) . . . . $125-$175

Shell Embossed—all colors (fig. 31) . . . . $125-$175

Shell & Seaweed—undecorated pink, blue, yellow (fig. 38) . . . . $90-$110

Shell & Seaweed—undecorated purple, green (fig. 36) . . . . $95-$125

Shell & Seaweed—enameled pink, blue, yellow (figs. 35, 37) . . . . $125-$175

Shell & Seaweed—enameled green, purple (fig. 34) . . . . $175-$225

Shell & Seaweed—Mother-of-Pearl, all colors (fig. 40) . . . . $175-$300

Shell & Seaweed—Rubina Verde enameled (fig. 41) . . . . $175-$225

Floral Embossed—pink, blue, yellow (fig. 42, left, 43) . . . . $125-$150

Floral Embossed—green, purple (fig. 42, right) . . . . $150-$175

Ribbed Satins—all colors, decorated and undecorated (fig. 44) . . . . $40-$65

Cherub decorated—all colors (fig. 48, 217, 372, 373) . . . . $150-$200

Souvenirs—pink, blue, yellow (figs. 49, 50, 51) . . . . $90-$125

Souvenirs—apricot, other uncommon colors (fig. 52) . . . . $125-$175

Souvenirs—white satin, decaled (figs. 53-56) . . . . $100-$150

Souvenirs—World's Fair, blue (fig. 59) . . . . $350-$450

Thomas Webb satin, Jules Barbe decoration—all colors (figs. 60, 64, 268) . . . .
. . . . $250-$325

MOP satin, diamond quilted, miniature—pink, blue, yellow (fig. 69) . . $275-$375

MOP satin, diamond quilted, T. Webb—pink, blue, yellow, off-white (figs. 70, 71)
. . . . $275-$325

MOP satin, diamond quilted—rainbow (figs. 72, 73) . . . . $600-$800

MOP satin, herringbone—blue, pink, yellow (figs. 75, 77) . . . . $110-$170

MOP satin, herringbone—apricot, white, etc. (figs. 76, 78, 79) . . . . $175-$250

MOP satin, ribbon—all colors, with and without wafer foot (figs. 81, 82, 83, 85) . .
. . . . $350-$450

MOP satin, ribbon—Coralene (fig. 84) . . . . $400-$500

MOP satin, ribbon, on base—all colors (figs. 86, 87) . . . . $400-$500

MOP satin, ribbon, tri-crimped—all colors (fig. 88) . . . . $400-$450
. . . . (undecorated, $150-$200)

Satin decorated, tri-crimped (fig. 90) . . . . $225-$275

Thomas Webb MOP satin, applied flowers—all colors, MINT (figs. 62, 63) . . . . . .
. . . . $300-$400

MOP satin, squat w/underplate—all colors (fig. 89) . . . . $400-$600

MOP satin, squat, no underplate—all colors (fig. 91) . . . . $200-$300

MOP satin swirl, Mt. Washington—all colors (fig. 92) . . . . $200-$250

MOP satin swirl, Mt. Washington, on base (fig. 93) . . . . $300-$350
Cut Velvet, diamond quilted—all colors (figs. 95-97, 99) . . . . $150-$250
Cut Velvet, stripe (fig. 98) . . . . $150-$250
S&W Box Pleated satin—all colors (figs. 100-102) . . . . $175-$275**
S&W Box pleated satin MOP, Pompeiian Swirl—all colors (figs. 108, 109) . . . . . .
. . . . $300-$600**
S&W box pleated Basketweave—all colors (figs. 112, 113) . . . . . . $300-$500**
MOP satin, decorated, other patterns—(figs. 104, 114-117) . . . . $500-$800
MOP cameo—all colors, crimped (fig. 119) . . . . $1200-$1400
more for box pleated Stevens & Williams
**more for colored interior*

1.2. Lusterless and White Satin

Lusterless—decoration in good condition (figs. 121-123) . . . . $75-$100
  (less for worn decoration)
White satin—decoration in good condition (figs. 127, 135) . . . . $75-$100
White satin—enameled (fig. 128-131) . . . . $95-$125

1.3. Albertine and Crown Milano

Crown Milano, unsigned, all designs and sizes (figs. 136-143, 147, 148) . $250-$350
Crown Milano, signed or with paper label, all designs and sizes (fig. 144) . . . .
. . . . $400-$500

1.4. Burmese

T. Webb, spherical, undecorated (fig. 271) . . . . $200-$250
T. Webb, spherical, decorated (fig. 155, 158, 159, 272) . . . . $300-$450
T. Webb, egg-style, decorated (fig. 156) . . . . $325-$475
T. Webb, egg-style, glossy, decorated (fig. 154) . . . . $400-$500
T. Webb, spherical, glossy, decorated (fig. 157) . . . . $400-$500

1.5. Peachblow

T. Webb, spherical, Jules Barbe decoration (fig. 162) . . . . $400-$600
T. Webb, spherical, undecorated (figs. 164, 166) . . . . $350-$450
T. Webb, egg-style, undecorated (fig. 167) . . . . $400-$500
World's Fair, undecorated (fig. 169) . . . . $250-$350
World's Fair, decorated (fig. 169) . . . . $350-$450

1.6. Spatter and Spangled Glass

Northwood Royal Ivy (fig. 171) . . . . $125-$175
Spherical spatter, rough pontils, mold seams—all colors (fig. 172) . . . . . . $20-$40
Tall spangled—all colors (fig. 173) . . . . $50-$70
Spatter basket (fig. 175) . . . . $200-$250
Spangled, spherical, monochromatic—blue, yellow, apricot (figs. 174, 176) . . . . . .
. . . . $100-$150
Spangled, applied glass toes, pink (fig. 177) . . . . $125-$175
Spangled, rainbow, spherical (fig. 178) . . . . $125-$175
Spangled spherical, green or purple (figs. 179, 180) $175-225
Spangled basket, tall (fig. 181) $190-225
Spangled, monochromatic, egg shape (fig. 183) . . . . $85-$100
Spangled, basket, applied cherries (fig. 182) . . . . $300-$325
Spangled basket, diamond quilted pattern (fig. 184) . . . . $300-$325
Spangled, spherical, striped (fig. 185) . . . . $75-$110

1.7. Bohemian Glass

"Greenies"—(fig. 186, 189) . . . . $60-$95
Moser egg-style miniature (fig. 188) . . . . $125-$175
Moser cranberry, 3 toes (fig. 187) . . . . $250-$300
Vaseline enameled (figs. 190-193, 195) . . . . $75-$125
Moser, clear, gold enamel, 3 toes, oversized (fig. 197) . . . . $350-$450
Moser, clear, gold enamel, 7" tall (fig. 196) . . . . $250-$275
Moser, intaglio engraved—amethyst, green (figs. 199, 200) . . . . $300-$400
Moser, shaded gold, enameled, Siamese (fig. 202) . . . . $400-$500
Moser (possible), light blue, enameled lily of the valley (fig. 203) . . . . $95-$145
Moser, enameled, rubena verde (fig. 204) . . . . $250-$275
Bohemian, gold and floral enameling (fig. 206) . . . . $85-$125
Bohemian, enameled, Caribbean blue (fig. 205) . . . . $125-$150
Bohemian, mottled, slightly iridescent translucent white (fig. 207) . . . . $45-$65
Bohemian, mottled, slightly iridescent translucent yellow to white (fig. 208) $55-$75
Lavender opalescent, gold scrollwork (fig. 209) . . . . $200-$225
Clear ribbed, gold enamel and scrollwork (fig. 210) . . . . $75-$100
Clear, orange enamel (fig. 211) . . . . $50-$80
Clear, nicely gilded, polished pontil (fig. 367) . . . . $75-$100 each
Shaded amethyst, enameled (figs. 212, 213) . . . . $75-$125
Cranberry enameled, miniature (fig. 214) . . . . $75-$110
Loetz, threaded (fig. 215) . . . . $250-$300
Pallme-Konig (fig. 216) . . . . $175-$250
Blue glossy, gold floral enamel (fig. 218) . . . . $65-$85
Iridescent, applied decoration (fig. 219) . . . . $145-$245
Basket, applied glass flowers (fig. 220, 221) . . . . $250-$275#
Spherical, applied glass flowers (fig. 222) . . . . $150-$200#
4-crimped, applied glass flower (fig. 223) . . . . $150-$200#
price for all flowers intact

1.8. Threaded Glass

Jewelled Glass, Zippers, miniatures—all colors (figs. 224-227) . . . . . . $125-$175
Jewelled Glass, Zipper, large spherical—all colors (figs. 231, 234) . . . . $110-$165
Jewelled Glass, Zipper, other shapes—all colors (fig. 233) . . . . $200-$250
Jewelled Glass, Raindrop, miniatures—all colors (figs. 228-230, 232) . . $135-$185
Jewelled Glass, Raindrop, large, heart shaped (fig. 235) . . . . $275-$325
Threaded, cranberry (figs. 236, 237) . . . . $95-$125
Osiris, with peacock eye MOP (fig. 239) . . . . $900-$1,000
Osiris, with raised herringbone pattern (figs. 238) . . . . $900-$1,000

1.9. Opalescent

Daisy & Fern (fig. 240, left) . . . . $65-$100
Spanish Lace (fig. 240, right) . . . . $75-$100
Spiral (fig. 242, 244) . . . . $50-$75
Spiral, Stevens & Williams (fig. 243) . . . . $150-$175
Fancy Fantails (fig. 245) . . . . $40-$75
Button Panels (fig. 246) . . . . $45-$55
Pearls and Scales (fig. 247) . . . . $65-$85

Daisy & Plume (fig. 248) . . . . $40-$60
Shell & Dots/Beaded Fan (fig. 249) . . . . $35-$45
Beaded Drapes (fig. 250) . . . . $40-$65
Piasa Bird (fig. 251) . . . . $65-$85
Blue opalescent, ribbed (fig. 253) . . . . $45-$55
Lavender opalescent, leaf pattern (fig. 254) . . . . $175-$225
Pink opalescent dot pattern (fig. 257) . . . . $80-$110
Blue to Vaseline, diamond pattern (fig. 256) . . . . $250-$300

1.10. Custard
Fine Cut & Roses (fig. 258) . . . . $75-$110
Beaded Cable . . . . $75-$85
Persian Medallion . . . . $50-$60

1.11. Li'l Guys
Tinies (fig. 260) . . . . $100-$150
MOP, pink diamond quilted, Coralene (fig. 264) . . . . $450-$550
MOP, diamond quilted—all colors (figs. 263, 265-267) . . . . $295-$400
T. Webb, Jules Barbe . . . . see satin glass
Custard, with acorns (fig. 273) . . . . $85-$110
Opalescent stripes (fig. 274) . . . . $100-$125
Cased—all colors (fig. 275) . . . . $100-$125
Satin—all colors (fig. 276) . . . . $115-$140
Clear, with needles and raised pine cone decoration (fig. 277) . . . . $125-$150
T, Webb, cameo, 4 crimped, collar base (fig. 278) . . . . $650-$800
Applied crystal petals/leaves (figs. 279, 280) . . . . $250-$300

1.12. Pattern Glass
Zippered Swirl & Diamond (figs. 294, 295) . . . . $45-$65
Roanoke (fig. 296) . . . . $25-$40
Tacoma (fig. 298) . . . . $35-$45
Duncan Block (fig. 297) . . . . $35-$50
Majestic (fig. 300) . . . . $65-$75
Banded Block (fig. 299) . . . . $10-$15
Robinson's Puritan (fig. 301) . . . . $35-$55
Fostoria's Victoria (fig. 303) . . . . $100-$150
Snail (fig. 302) . . . . $65-$75
Thumbprint (fig. 307) . . . . $35-$45
Cube and Fan (figs. 306, 308) . . . . $20-$35
Isabella Saratoga (fig. 309) . . . . $20-$35

1.13. Miscellaneous
Cut (fig. 311) . . . . $250-$300
Porcelain (figs. 312-314, 317—See Section 2)
Mat-Su-No-Ke (figs. 315, 316, 318, 319) . . . .
    $700-$1100, depending on size, color
Custard, house scenes painted, florals (figs. 320, 323) . . . . $100-$145
Zipper copy (fig. 325) . . . . $60-$85
Goddess (fig. 327) . . . . $95-$125

Cup "Saucer" (fig. 328) . . . . $250-$300
Opaline "Saturn" (fig. 330) . . . . $95-$125
Pink, white frosted swirl (fig. 329) . . . . $250-$300
Rubena Royal Ivy (fig. 332) . . . . $125-$165
Rubena, Emil Stanger, ribbed (fig. 331) . . . . $75-$110
Rubena, fine DQ pattern (fig. 333) . . . . $75-$110
Camphor (figs. 334, 335) . . . . $30-$45
S&W white swirl (fig. 336) . . . . $95-$135
Overshot (fig. 337) . . . . $145-$175
Decorated with figures, light colored (figs. 340, 341, 344) . . . . $150-$200
Decal floral (fig. 342) . . . . $75-$95
Vaseline opal stripe, applied flowers (fig. 345) . . . . . $125-$175 (all flowers intact)
Bi-colored, decorated with floral (fig. 346) . . . . $110-$135
Fancy blue, applied glass (fig. 350) . . . . $145-$195
Cranberry with underplate (fig. 352) . . . . $95-$150
Hobnail basket (fig. 353) . . . . $145-$195
Peloton (figs. 355-357) . . . . $200-$300
Spherical, decorated with portrait, Indian (fig. 359) . . . . $165-$210
Nailsea (fig. 358) . . . . $195-$245
Graniteware/Venetian (figs. 362, 363, 365) . . . . $45-$85
Hobnail, blown (figs. 360, 361) . . . . $75-$125
Frosted, Coralene (fig. 360) . . . . $145-$165

2.1. Carnival
(M-Marigold, A-Amethyst, B-Blue, G-Green, AO-Aqua Opalescent)
Beaded Cable (fig. 374-377) . . . . . . $110-$140M, $90-$150A, $150-$200B, $275-$300G, $250-$350AO
Dugan Grape Delight (fig. 380) . . . . $70-$125 all colors
L.G. Wright Grape (fig. 381) . . . . $40-$50
Star and File (fig. 382) . . . . $75M, $125-$175, A or G
Louisa (fig. 385) . . . . $80-$115 all colors
Imperial Grape (fig. 384) . . . . $100-$200 all colors, $600 amber
Orange Tree (fig. 387) . . . . $75-$125 all colors
Leaf and Beads (fig. 388) . . . . $385-$425 AO, $125-$250—all colors except ice blue
Concave Flute (figs. 386, 390) . . . . $150-$225
Drapery (fig. 391) . . . . $350M, $550-$700 ice blue, $$600 white, $175 A or G
Swirl Hobnail (fig. 392) . . . . $300-$600
Fenton Swirl Hobnail (fig. 393) . . . . $20-$30
Daisy & Plume (figs. 394, 397) . . . . $75-$120 M, A, B, G, $175 PO
Garland (fig. 395) . . . . $75-$110 M, B, $300 A
Two Flowers (fig. 396) . . . . $195-$250
Wreath of Roses (fig. 399) . . . . $50-$75
Fine Cut and Roses (figs. 398, 400) . . . . $175-$275 M, A, G, B

2.2. Depression Glass
Caprice (fig. 401) . . . . $125-$160 blue
Canterbury (figs. 402-404) . . . . crystal, $10-$15, opalescent, $50-$125
Omero (fig. 406) . . . . $150-$20
Duncan & Miller hobnail, stemmed (fig. 405) . . . . $15-$20

McKee (fig. 407) . . . . $35-$55
Tourjours (fig. 408) . . . . $55-$75
American (fig. 409) . . . . $10-$20
Molly, all colors (figs. 410) . . . . $25-$40
Baroque (fig. 415) . . . . $55-$105
Jubilee blank (fig. 416) . . . . $15-$25

2.3. American Art Glass
Durand (fig. 417) . . . . $725-$1325
Imperial Free Hand (fig. 418) . . . . $1400-$1600
Fenton Beaded Melon (fig. 420) . . . . $5-$75
Fenton opalescent hobnail (fig. 422) . . . . $45-$95

2.4. European Art Glass
Rossler, all colors (figs. 423-427) . . . . $125-$175, amethyst, $200
Mini Rossler-style blank, possible Moser enamel (figs. 428, 429) . . . . . $225-$275
Mini, frosted cranberry, sailboat (fig. 430) . . . . $65-$85
Mini, green, ribbed (fig. 432) . . . . $65-$85
Mini, cranberry (fig. 433) . . . . $65-$85
Mini milk, no crimps, flora, Czecho Slovakia (fig. 434) . . . . $10-$15
Loetz Tango Glass, Dagobert Pesche (fig. 435) . . . . $2000-$2500
Orrefors (figs. 436, 437) . . . . $45-$95
French cameo (figs. 441-450) . . . . $200-$400
Paperweight style (fig. 453) . . . . $35-$65
Bagerly (figs. 451, 452) . . . . $10-$20

2.5. Ceramic Rose Bowls
Austrian Porcelain (fig. 312) . . . . $45-$65
Think of me (fig. 313) . . . . $45-$65
Schiller—looks like wood (fig. 300) . . . . $100-$125
Lighthouse (fig. 317) . . . . $150-$200
RC Bavaria (fig. 454) . . . . $45-$65
Miniature, advertising (fig. 455) . . . . $35-$55
TK Czechoslovakia (fig. 456) . . . . $75-$110
EIAPG (fig. 457) . . . . $45-$65
Spring Light (fig. 458) . . . . $65-$95
Oriental, deep crimps (fig. 460) . . . . $65-$95
Oriental, 6 peaked crimps (fig. 463) . . . . $50-$75
Orchid, Germany (figs. 461, 462) . . . . $75-$100
Misc. china (figs. 464-472) . . . . $45-$65

3.1. L.G. Wright
Wright peachblow, undecorated (fig. 473) . . . . $55-$75
Wright peachblow, decorated (fig. 476) . . . . $75-$110
Tortoiseshell (fig. 474) . . . . $35-$45
Daisy & Fern (fig. 478) . . . . $65-$95
Maize (fig. 480) . . . . $85-$125
Eye Dot (fig. 481) . . . . $85-$105
Thumbprint (figs. 479, 482) . . . . $65-$95
Wright Opal Open (fig. 484) . . . . $25-$35

Decorated overlay (fig. 485) . . . . $75-$110
Puffed rose overlay (fig. 486) . . . . $35-$55
Daisy & Button, all colors (fig. 488) . . . . $15-$35
Mary Gregory (fig. 491) . . . . $65-$85
Hobnail, tight crimps (fig. 487) . . . . $25-$40
Amberina honeycomb (fig. 492) . . . . $25-$35
Opalescent stripe/Graniteware minis (fig. 493-495) . . . . $75-$125
Priscilla (fig. 496) . . . . $25-$45

3.2. Italian Reproductions
Pink satin (fig. 498) . . . . $35-$45
MOP, pink, blue, yellow (figs. 502, 505, 506) . . . . $45-$85
MOP, other colors (figs. 502-504, 507) . . . . $55-$95
MOP rainbow (fig. 501) . . . . $100-$150
Swag design, applied feet (fig. 508) . . . . $95-$145
Spatter (fig. 509) . . . . $55-$75
Nailsea (fig. 510) . . . . $55-$65
Aventurine (figs. 512, 513) . . . . $65-$75
Burmese (fig. 511) . . . . $45-$60
Burmese decorated (figs. 515) . . . . $55-$70
Peachblow (fig. 511, back right) . . . . $45-$60
Plated amberina (fig. 518) . . . . $60-$75

3.3 Italian Originals
Latticino (figs. 519, 520) . . . . $125-$150
Applied rigaree (fig. 522) . . . . $75-$95
Stemmed, swag design (fig. 523) . . . . $45-$55

3.4. Japanese Repros
Satin (fig. 524) . . . . $35-$45 (unusual colors, $65-$85)
Cranberry (fig. 527) . . . . $45-$55
Reddish translucent (fig. 529) . . . . $30-$40
Dot cut-to-clear (fig. 530) . . . . $40-$50
Rose cut-to-clear (fig. 531, 532) current retail, about $25

3.5. American Burmese/Peachblow Repros
Bennett peachblow (fig. 533) . . . . $45-$65

3.6. Fenton's Late Models
Leaf Decorated Burmese (fig. 534) . . . . $65-$85
Mary Walrath Love Bouquet Burmese (fig. 535) . . . . $75-$95
Circle of Love Burmese (fig. 537)—too limited, too new. No data
Burmese Poppy (fig. 536) . . . . $50-$60
One in the Spirit (figs. 538, 539)—too limited. No data.
Hanging Hearts (figs. 540, 541) . . . . $85-$120
Fine Dot (fig. 542) . . . . $50-$85
Beatty Honeycomb (fig. 543) . . . . $45-$60
Snowflake (fig. 547) . . . . $65-$85
Drapery (fig. 548) . . . . $45-$55
Toed, egg shape hobnail (fig. 549) . . . . $5-$10
Other Poppy (fig. 550) . . . . $35-$50

Footed pink, decal (fig. 551) . . . . $45-$70
Plum Carnival (fig. 553) . . . . $55-$75
75th Jubilee purple (fig. 552) . . . . $65-$85
Lily of the Valley—all colors (fig. 556) . . . . $20-$30
Rosalene (fig. 554) . . . . $75-$85
Decorated overlay (fig. 555) . . . . $45-$55
Modern "pattern" glass (fig. 559) . . . . $20-$35
Wild Horses (figs. 557, 558) . . . . $140-$165
Unicorn (fig. 560) . . . . $140-$165

3.7. Miscellaneous Late Models

Czech hobnail—all colors, no crimps (fig. 562) . . . . $20-$30
Czech Cut (fig. 561) . . . .$65-$85
Lefton china (fig. 563) . . . . $25-$40
Diana Art Studio (fig. 564) . . . . $15-$25
Belleek (fig. 565) . . . . $40-$65
Gibson's Staffordshire (fig. 566) . . . . $35-$45
Limoges (fig. 567) . . . . $65-$95
Colored milk glass (fig. 568, 569) . . . . $20-$30
Imperial Carnival (fig. 570) . . . . $30-$40
Blenko—all colors (fig. 575) . . . . $35-$50
Intaglio (figs. 576, 577) . . . . $35-$50
English Hobnail, pedestal (fig. 579) . . . . $10-$20
Pairpoint (fig. 581) . . . . $25 currently at factory
Crackle (fig. 578) . . . . $30-$45
Amethyst Rose Bowl Lady (fig. 582) . . . . Priceless
Miniature, clear, custom-made (fig. 583) . . . . Priceless

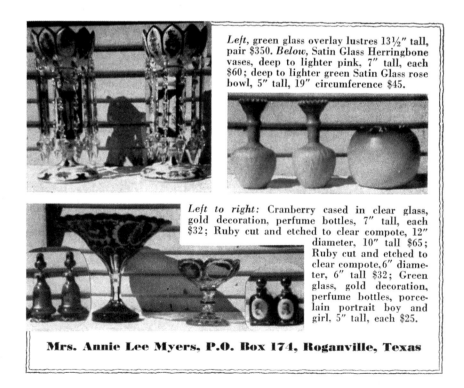

Fig. 586. Vintage antique ad offering rose bowls for sale.

BIBLIOGRAPHY

Antique & Collectors Reproduction News,
Sept. 1998, Nov. 1997, Jan. 1996, Sept.
1996, Sept. 1995, Oct. 1994, Feb. 1994,
Nov. 1992, Aug. 1993, Dec. 1992.

Archer, Margaret & Douglas. *Imperial Glass.*
Paducah, KY: Collector Books, 1978.

Avila, George C., *The Pairpoint Glass Story.*
New Bedford, MA: Reynolds-DeWalt
Printing, Inc., 1968.

Baker, Gary E., Holly Hoover McCluskey,
Jane Shadel Spillman, G. Eason Eige,
James S. Measell and Kenneth M. Wilson.
Wheeling Glass: 1829-1939. Wheeling,
WV: Collection of the Oglebay Institute
Glass Museum, Oblebay Institute, 1994.

Baldwin, Gary. *Moser Artistic Glass.* 2d ed.
Marietta, OH: Antique Publications,
1997.

Barlow, Raymond E. and Joan E. Kaiser. *A
Guide to Sandwich Glass.* Windham, NH:
Barlow-Kaiser Publishing Company, Inc.,
1985.

Barret, Richard Carter. *Identification of
American Art Glass,* 1964.

Bredehoft, Neila & Tom. Hobbs, Brockunier
& Co. Glass. *Identification and Value
Guide.* Paducah, KY: Collector Books,
1997.

Edwards, Bill and Mike Carwile. *Standard
Encyclopedia of Carnival Glass.* 6th ed.
Paducah, KY: Collector Books, 1998.

Edwards, Bill. *Standard Encyclopedia of
Opalescent Glass.* 2d ed. Paducah, KY:
Collector Books, 1997.

Eige, Eason and Rick Wilson. *Blenko Glass:
1930-1953.* Marietta, OH: Antique
Publications, 1987.

Florence, Gene. *Elegant Glassware of the
Depression Era.* 5th ed. Paducah, KY:
Collector Books, 1993.

Gardner, Paul V. *The Glass of Frederick
Carder.* New York, NY: Crown
Publishers, Inc., 1971.

Glickman, Jay L. *Yellow-Green Vaseline. A
Guide to the Magic Glass.* Marietta, OH:
Antique Publications, 1991.

Glickman, Jay L. *Yellow-Green Vaseline. A
Guide to the Magic Glass.* Rev. ed.
Marietta, OH: Antique Publications,
1998.

Hajdamach, Charles R. *British Glass: 1800-
1914.* Woodbridge, Suffolk, England:
Antique Collector's Club, 1991.

Hammond, Dorothy. *Confusing Collectibles.*
Des Moines, IA: Wallace-Homestead,
1972.

Hammond, Dorothy. *More Confusing
Collectibles.* Vol. 2. Wichita, KS: C.B.P.
Publishing, 1972.

Heacock, William. *1000 Toothpick Holders.*
Marietta, OH: Antique Publications,
1977.

Heacock, William, *Collecting Glass.* Vol. 3.
Marietta, OH: Antique Publications,
1986.

Heacock, William. *Toothpick Holders from
A to Z,* 2d. ed., bk. 1, *Encyclopedia of
Victorian Colored Pattern Glass.*
Marietta, OH: Antique Publications,
1976.

Heacock, William. *Opalescent Glass from A
to Z,* bk. 2, *Encyclopedia of Victorian
Colored Pattern Glass.* Marietta, OH:
Antique Publications, 1975.

Heacock, William. *Syrups, Sugar Shakers and
Cruets from A to Z,* bk. 3, *Encyclopedia
of Victorian Colored Pattern Glass.*
Marietta, OH: Antique Publications,
1976.

Heacock, William. *Custard Glass from A to
Z,* bk. 4, *Encyclopedia of Victorian
Colored Pattern Glass.* Marietta, OH:
Antique Publications, 1976.

Heacock, William. *U.S. Glass from A to Z,*
bk. 5, *Encyclopedia of Victorian Colored
Pattern Glass.* Marietta, OH: Antique
Publications, 1978.

Heacock, William. *Oil Cruets from A to Z,*
bk. 6, *Encyclopedia of Victorian Colored
Pattern Glass.* Marietta, OH: Antique
Publications, 1981.

Heacock, William. *Ruby-Stained Glass from
A to Z,* bk. 7, *Encyclopedia of Victorian
Colored Pattern Glass.* Marietta, OH:
Antique Publications, 1986.

Heacock, William and William Gamble.
Cranberry Opalescent from A to Z, bk. 9,
*Encyclopedia of Victorian Colored
Pattern Glass.* Marietta, OH: Antique
Publications, 1987.

Heacock, William. *Fenton Glass: The First
Twenty-Five Years.* Marietta, OH:
Antique Publications, 1978.

Heacock, William. *Fenton Glass: The Second
Twenty-Five Years.* Marietta, OH:
Antique Publications, 1980.

Heacock, William. *Fenton Glass: The Third
Twenty-Five Years.* Marietta, OH:
Antique Publications, 1989.

Heacock, William, James Measell, Berry
Wiggins. *Dugan/Diamond: The Story of
Indiana, Pennsylvania Glass.* Marietta,
OH: Antique Publications, 1993.

Husfloen, Kyle. *American & European
Decorative & Art Glass Price Guide.*
Dubuque, IA: Antique Trader Books,
1994.

Husfloen, Kyle. *Collector's Guide to
American Pressed Glass: 1825-1915.*
Radnor, PA: Wallace-Homestead, 1992.

Jenks, Bill, and Jerry Luna. *Early American
Pattern Glass. 1850-1910.* Radnor, PA:
Homestead, 1990.

Kovar, Lorraine. *Westmoreland Glass: 1950-
1984.* Marietta, OH: Antique
Publications, 1991.

Kovar, Lorraine. *Westmoreland Glass: 1950-1984*. Vol. 2. Marietta, OH: Antique Publications, 1991.

Lagerberg, Ted and Vi. *A Color Picture Guide to Over 100 Types of Collectible Glass*. Bk 2. New Port Richey, FL: Modern Photographers, 1966.

Lagerberg, Ted and Vi, with C.C. Manley. *Collectible Glass, Bk 4, British Glass*. New Port Richey, FL: Modern Photographers, 1968.

Lee, Ruth Webb. *Antique Fakes & Reproductions*. Wellesley Hills, MA: Lee Publications, 1938.

Lee, Ruth Webb. *Early American Pressed Glass*. Wellesley Hills, MA: Lee Publications, 1931.

Lee, Ruth Webb. *Nineteenth-Century Art Glass*. New York, NY: M. Barrows & Company, Inc., 1952.

Manley, C.C. "Czech-Baroque Glass," *Spinning Wheel*, May 1969.

Manley, Cyril. *Decorative Victorian Glass*. New York, NY: Van Nostrand Reinhold Company, 1981.

McCain, Mollie Helen. *The Collector's Encyclopedia of Pattern Glass*. Paducah, KY: Collector Books, 1982.

Measell, James, ed. *Fenton Glass: The 1980s Decade*. Marietta, OH: Antique Publications, 1996.

Measell, James and W.C. "Red" Rotteis. *The L.G. Wright Glass Company*. Marietta, OH: Antique Publications, 1997.

Mebane, John. *Collecting Bride's Baskets and Other Glass Fancies*, Des Moines, IA: Wallace-Homestead, 1976.

Meschi, Edward J. *Durand: The Man and His Glass*. Marietta, OH: Antique Publications, 1998.

Murray, Melvin, L. *Fostoria, Ohio Glass II*. Marietta, OH: Antique Publications, n.d.

Peterson, Arthur G., Ph.D. *400 Trademarks on Glass*. Gas City, IN: L-W Book Sales, 1968.

Pina, Leslie. *Fostoria: Serving the American Table 1887-1986*. Atglen, PA: Schiffer Publishing, 1995.

Pina, Leslie, and Jerry Gallagher. *Tiffin Glass: 1914-1940*. Atglen, PA: Schiffer Publishing, 1996.

Pullin, Anne Geffken. *Glass Signatures, Trademarks and Tradenames*. Radnor, PA: Wallace-Homestead, 1986.

Revi, Albert Christian, "The Gundersen-Pairpoint Glass Works: Burmese, Peach Blow, Rose Amber," *Spinning Wheel*, Sept. 1962.

Revi, Albert Christian. *Nineteenth Century Glass: Its Genesis and Development*. Rev. ed. Exton, PA: Schiffer Publishing, 1967.

Revi, Albert Christian, ed. *Spinning Wheel's Collectible Glass*. Castle Books, 1974.

Revi, Albert Christian, "Threaded Glassware," *Spinning Wheel*, July 1958.

Shuman III, John A. *The Collector's Encyclopedia of American Art Glass*. Paducah, KY: Collector Books, 1988.

Stoudt, Sandra. *Heisey on Parade*. Lombard, IL: Wallace-Homestead, 1985.

Teal, Sr., Ron. *Albany Glass: Model Flint Glass Company of Albany, Indiana*. Marietta, OH: Antique Publications, 1997.

Truitt, Robert & Deborah. *Collectible Bohemian Glass: 1880-1940*. Kensington, MD: B&D Glass, 1995.

Van Tassel, Valentine, "The Queen Ordered Burmese," *The Antiques Journal*, Nov. 1952.

Watkins, Laura Woodside. *Cambridge Glass: 1818-1888*. New York, NY: Bramhall House, 1930.

Weatherman, Hazel Marie. *Colored Glassware of the Depression Era*. Springfield, MO: Hazel Marie Weatherman, 1970.

Weatherman, Hazel Marie. *Colored Glassware of the Depression Era 2*. Ozark, MO: Weatherman Glassbooks, 1974.

"Who Knows?" *Spinning Wheel*, Aug. 1958, no author listed.

Wilson, Chas West. *Westmoreland Glass. Identification & Value Guide*. Paducah, KY: Collector Books, 1996.

Woodward, H.W. *Art, Feat and Mystery. The Story of Thomas Webb & Sons, Glassmakers*. Stourbridge, West Midlands, England: Mark + Moody Limited, 1978.

Yeakley, Virginia and Loren. *Heisey Glass in Color*. Bk 2. Newark, OH: Virginia and Loren Yeakley, 1978.

INDEX

ABOUT THE AUTHORS

Johanna S. and Sean Billings bought their first rose bowl in 1992, intending to give the blue satin example to a family member. But by the time they got it home that day, they couldn't part with it. Since then, their rose bowl passion has grown, leading to a large and varied collection, the founding of the Rose Bowl Collectors club in 1994, and finally this book.

Johanna is an award-winning writer/photographer whose work has been published in many popular magazines. With the help of Sean, she does a regular column for *Antique Week* answering reader questions about old glass. They are vetters for the Atlantique City show and Johanna also serves as an advisor for *Warman's Antiques & Collectibles Price Guide*. She was also recently appointed editor to the Mt. Washington Art Glass Society newsletter.

In addition to writing about antiques and collectibles, Johanna has done pieces on various topics for popular magazines such as *Cat Fancy, Redbook, Reader's Digest and Business Start-Ups*. She has done public relations and publicity writing for KidsPeace Corp. and the National Canal Museum and volunteered her writing talents to help Bill & Marie Guthier of Coopersburg, Pennsylvania, raise $250,000 for a lung transplant for their daughter. Johanna and Sean also volunteer for Good Mews, a Lehigh Valley, Pennsylvania, non-profit organization which places homeless cats.

In 1996, Johanna graduated summa cum laude with a bachelor's degree in English. Sean graduated in 1997 from Temple University.

In addition to rose bowls, Sean has a growing collecting of ring vases, Smith Brothers, and Mt. Washington glass. He is interested in industrial as well as glass history and is an active member of and volunteer for the Walnutport Canal Association. He is also a member of Hugh Moore Park and the National Canal Museum, the Wayne County Historical Society, the Pennsylvania Canal Society, and the American Canal Society.

Johanna and Sean live in Danielsville, Pennsylvania, with their daughter Kayleigh, three cats, and a growing collection of glass.